Lindis- Chloe ☑ P9-AFQ-260
from Cathy Whyte March 2010
Shri Aurobindo Ashram

Empower Women

Empower Women

AN AWAKENING

Leena Chawla Rajan

RADHA SOAMI SATSANG BEAS

*Be the change you want
to see in the world.*
Mahatma Gandhi

Published by:
J. C. Sethi, Secretary
Radha Soami Satsang Beas
Dera Baba Jaimal Singh
Punjab 143 204, India

© 2010 Radha Soami Satsang Beas
All rights reserved

First edition 2010

17 16 15 14 13 12 11 10   8 7 6 5 4 3 2 1

ISBN 978-81-8256-885-3

Printed in India by: Lakshmi Offset Printers

CONTENTS

Foreword

Somebody's got to stop the rot,
so why not you?
Lawrence School Sanawar,
school song

Empower Women is not intended as a book in the ordinary sense. It is rather a measured response to a grave situation in our society today. The increasing practice of sex-selection by killing female infants in the womb is a manifestation of a fundamental flaw in our perception and treatment of women. It is also a manifestation of our blindness to the spiritual foundation and fundamental law of life – the law of karma, of cause and effect.

The book provokes us to think, to bring our actions in tune with the spiritual and moral obligations we have as members of society. To do this, we need to change our attitudes drastically. The authors have tried to give facts and figures interspersed with real life stories and experiences to impress upon us the need for this change in attitude.

The book looks at the role of woman in the grand scheme of life and how the present situation is an outcome of centuries of misguided thinking that women are inferior to men. It is equally the outcome of our failure to take responsibility for what we do. So while the phenomenon of sex-selection and female foeticide is recognized in present-day India as wrong, unlawful, immoral, sinful, and nationally unacceptable, no one is ready to take responsibility for the unfolding crisis. It is easy to blame others so that in the end, no one feels responsible. The law of karma, however, will inevitably take its course. As you sow, so you reap: this world is a field of karmas. If we sow seeds of violence, we shall reap violence; if we cause suffering, we shall suffer. Responsibility is apportioned by the law of karmic accountability, and in the context of sex-selection and the ongoing suffering of women, we are all responsible.

Traditional patriarchal practices in India have given us a male-dominated society where it is the man's perceptions and mindset which lay the foundation of our social order. If a man projects a woman in the role of mother or sister, she is elevated, respected and even worshipped. If he sees her with lustful eyes, and his lust produces consequences, she is branded by society as the temptress while not an iota of blame goes to him. This male-dominated projection of life has to change, for it distorts reality, and an awakening is needed so life is seen for what it is. Since in our society, power lies mostly with men, the onus of change too lies first and foremost with men.

The situation with regard to sex-selection is going from bad to worse. Drastic measures and an immediate response are called for if we want a better world for our future generations. For the right response, we need to understand and tackle not just the phenomenon – sex-selection – but the root cause, the inequality of women in our society. *Empower Women* does not propose going from one extreme to another by advocating the domination of women over men. Rather it envisages a new and better world that comes from true equality between the sexes, and from a healthy balance where men and women respect the strengths of each other and are tolerant of each other's weaknesses. By changing our attitudes towards women each one of us can play a part in uprooting this social and spiritual evil from our lives and our society. The choice is ours.

G. S. Dhillon
December 2009

Introduction

Desh mrinmoy noi, desh chinmoy.
The nation is not a chunk of earth:
it is a saga of consciousness.

Rabindranath Tagore

This slender book is a call to action. It urges us to take a realistic look at the choices and contradictions that are shaping our present-day society and the terrible suffering endured by women.

On one hand, ours is considered to be a very spiritual nation. Here we will find a temple, mosque, gurudwara or church at every street corner. Here we will find the greatest concentration of vegetarians in the world. This is the country that gained its independence through non-violent means and exported the concept abroad. We have deep-rooted spiritual traditions which go back centuries.

On the other hand, we live in a society where women are treated very poorly. Girls are so unwanted that many millions are aborted in the womb or killed right after birth. After they are born, they struggle through a childhood in which they are second-class citizens. Young girls are deprived of the same nutrition, education and opportunities their brothers receive. Many are married off in their early teens; and to get girls married parents have to pay the in-laws a dowry which is often far beyond their means. As a result, girls are considered to be an unbearable burden. Most women are financially dependent and socially conditioned from childhood to consider themselves inferior. Many are physically and emotionally abused.

On the one hand we worship women: we go to a temple and pray to the goddesses Laxmi, Saraswati and Durga Mata; we revere motherhood to the extent that we call the planet we live on 'Mother Earth', and our nation 'our motherland'. Yet we think nothing of eliminating a child's life just because she is a girl. Can a spiritual nation treat half its population with such callousness? We read in our scriptures that all are equal, that God is love, and that we must love all in his creation; yet we love our sons and withhold that love from our daughters.

Do we not see the contradictions in our actions?

Empowering women is a subject with a very broad scope. Without a doubt government and non-government organizations have done a lot to improve women's education, health, nutrition and safety, and will continue to work tirelessly in this area. This systemic response to the broad issue of women's empowerment is not the focus of the book. *Empower Women* focuses, instead, on a very different and crucial point – *that true societal change begins with the individual*. As the crisis caused by sex-selection unfolds around us, what is our understanding of the issue and what is our individual response? We, as individuals, matter because individuals make families, and families are the fundamental building blocks of society.

Proposing an awakening, the book calls for clear thinking and compassion, saying that both these qualities are intrinsic to who we really *are*. India's beloved poet, Rabindranath Tagore, tells us that our country is not a chunk of earth, it is a saga of consciousness. We are all part of this collective consciousness; we are all intricately intertwined and connected to one another. The choices we make shape both our lives and the world we pass on to our children.

Empower Women urges us to look deep into our conscience and judge whether our treatment of women is morally or spiritually acceptable. It suggests that far from being a burden, women are among creation's most precious treasures and urges us to empower them.

1

VALUING THE WOMEN
IN OUR LIVES

A woman is the full circle.
Within her is the power to create,
nurture and transform.

Diane Mariechild

A woman has many facets, and she plays many roles in life, each one special and unique.

Her role in society

Women play a key role in upholding our culture. Through the ages, women have told their children stories which they heard from their mothers; mythology and folklore exist today mainly because women have upheld the oral tradition. From the folk songs we sing to the traditional dances we perform, from the clothes we wear and the food we eat to the rituals we perform at festivals and holidays – women play a key role in passing down our rich heritage from one generation to the next. It is through these traditions that women perpetuate the values that hold family and society together.

At times of war, when hundreds of thousands of men are eliminated at one time, it is the women who cope, who despite great hardship hold the community together. It is the women who tend the sick and wounded, take care of the elderly, provide for their children, and train the next generation to take over. Women create continuity down the generations; they are the very backbone of a secure society.

> The fastest way to change society is to mobilize the women of the world.
>
> *Charles Malik, former President,*
> *United Nations General Assembly*

As more and more women in India exercise their right to vote, their voices are beginning to count and their issues are being heard. Today, women are seen in all walks of public life – in the administrative services, in the police force, as lawyers, judges and powerful politicians. Women in the media are visible examples of the change women can bring about in society. Women are seen in large numbers in the area of social work. Many government and non-government organizations are headed by women who care enough to bring about change on issues ranging from the welfare of our children to the future of our environment.

Her role in the economy

In addition to their crucial role in society, women play an integral role in the economy. There are many homes that would not survive without the earning potential of its women. In days gone by, what a woman could do was somewhat determined and limited by her physical strength. It took strength to hunt an animal, to pull a plough or to fight a war. Therefore, quite naturally, a woman's role evolved around tasks that were equally important but needed less strength.

But the world has changed. We are now in the Global Information Age and physical strength is no longer a primary factor in most jobs. There is almost nothing a woman cannot do if she is given equal opportunity. In India today, women are doctors, lawyers, judges, politicians, entrepreneurs, engineers and scientists. Women are excelling in art, in sports and in the media. Women are in the defence forces and in the police force. Today, a woman can lead a country, drive a tractor, or pilot a spacecraft to the moon!

Increasingly, research studies are proving that women add a very unique value in the workplace.[1] Studies show that women leaders are persuasive and willing to take risks; they can be assertive, make quick decisions, articulate a vision and rally a team around it; they are empathetic, flexible and have strong interpersonal skills. Women are able to multi-task effectively. Women tend to bring others around to their point of view because they genuinely understand and care about where others are coming from so that the people they are leading feel more understood, supported and valued. They tend to be more stable, less turf-conscious and seek less personal glory. They are more likely to share information with their employees rather than dispensing it on a need-to-know basis.

> Women get high ratings on exactly those skills needed to succeed in the Global Information Age, where teamwork and partnering are so important.
>
> *Rosabeth Moss Kanter, Harvard Business School Professor*

More and more companies are now making increasing use of the feminine style of management, not just because it is ethical to employ an equal number of women or because they have a legal obligation to do so, but because it benefits their business.

Her role in the family

Imagine what life would be like without a grandmother's childhood stories, a mother's selfless love, or a wife's lifelong companionship? What would life be like without a sister's teasing affection, or a daughter to shower us with love and hugs? Nurturing and caring, full of joy and love, brimming over with all the feminine qualities so special to them…what would our families be like without women?

God has entrusted woman with a special responsibility, a special gift. She is *janani*: one who has the unique ability to renew life on earth as she bears children.

> That special power of loving that belongs to a woman is seen most clearly when she becomes a mother. Motherhood is a gift of God to women.
>
> *Mother Teresa*

A woman bears children with joy, despite the tremendous risk, physical pain and emotional upheaval involved. And she nurtures her children selflessly. When there is a shortage of food, she feeds her children and goes hungry herself; when they get hurt, she is there to bandage and kiss it better; when they are sick, she stays up night after night to nurse them back to health. If they are unhappy or in pain, she can never be at ease. Day after day, tirelessly, a mother pays attention to her children's well-being: what they are eating, how they are growing, who their friends are, how they are feeling. Even if they were to turn their back on her, a mother's love would remain constant.

> Who is it that loves me and will love me forever with an affection which no chance, no misery, no crime of mine can take away? It is you, my mother.
>
> *Thomas Carlyle*

It has been rightly said: there is no earthly love which is as pure and as selfless as a mother's love for her children.

> God could not be everywhere, and therefore he created mothers.
>
> *Jewish proverb*

A woman is the child's first and arguably most influential teacher. In most cultures around the world, women spend the maximum time with their children, especially in the early years. A woman teaches her children to speak and understand their native language, their 'mother tongue'. She helps them with their schoolwork. She teaches them the most important values of life. She moulds and influences their character, habits and personality; she influences their beliefs, biases and prejudices.

> One good mother is worth a hundred schoolmasters.
>
> *George Herbert*

An educated, happy and secure mother imparts not just academic teaching, but also a sense of well-being and security to her children.

The future destiny of the child is always the work of the mother.

Napoleon Bonaparte

My mother was the most beautiful woman…All I am I owe to my mother…I attribute all my success in life to the moral, intellectual and physical education I received from her.

George Washington

Women quite effortlessly bring warmth, love, cleanliness, order and beauty to a home. Women teach us courtesy and good manners. Women show us how to communicate effectively within the family and with the larger community in which we live.

What is truly indispensable for the conduct of life has been taught us by women – the small rules of courtesy, the actions that win us the warmth of deference of others; the words that assure us a welcome; the attitudes that must be varied to mesh with character or situation; all social strategy.

Rémy de Gourmont

Women are loyal companions to their husbands in good times and in bad. Not only is a woman loving toward her own parents, she forges strong bonds with her husband's family as well. Women make an effort to reach out to the extended family and they unite families by creating a strongly woven tapestry of relationships. Women nurture not just children, they also take care of the elderly and the sick.

A woman is the key to a happy and peaceful home. In fact, it is a woman who *makes* a home.

Her unique feminine qualities

Traditionally, there are certain personality traits which are considered to be masculine: strength, aggression, independence, territorialism, dominance, leadership, rationalism, courage. Similarly there are certain traits which are considered to be essentially feminine: intuition, patience, gentleness, empathy, tolerance, expressiveness, kindness, sacrificial love.

This is not to say that men have only masculine traits and women have only feminine traits; they both have masculine and feminine traits in different proportions. What determines the proportions? One factor is genetic. Scientific studies have now proved, for example, that because of the way a woman's brain is wired, she is more intuitive. Similarly, a male is naturally more territorial, as has been displayed over time in both human and animal behaviour.

Another factor is social conditioning. Young children are taught that "boys don't cry." From the very outset, young men are trained and conditioned to be aggressive and to repress qualities like kindness and empathy, because these are perceived to be more 'weak' and 'feminine'. Similarly, girls are taught from childhood that meekness and endless sacrifice are desirable and expected traits in women. If a man exhibits a particular behaviour he is called confident; if a woman exhibits the same behaviour she is considered unattractively aggressive. Over time, such relentless social conditioning cements certain masculine and feminine qualities in us.

The truth, however, is that the most successful and fulfilled men are those who are most 'whole'; those who have been allowed to develop both their masculine and feminine sides. The same is true of women.

Another reality is that, in nature, feminine qualities are essential to balance masculine qualities. If there were only masculine qualities – in an individual, in a nation, or in the world – there would be more war, aggression and chaos than currently exists. Women are not just valuable, their feminine qualities are essential for creating harmony and balance in society.

Women add immeasurable value
to our families,
to our communities,
and to the world.
We could not live a complete
and enriched life
without them.

2

HER CURRENT CONDITION

> *You can tell the condition of a nation*
> *by looking at the status of its women.*
> Jawaharlal Nehru

If we were to judge the condition of our nation by looking at the status of our women, what would we find? Since independence, great strides have been made in the areas of women's health and literacy. Today, we have female politicians, entrepreneurs, doctors, lawyers, engineers and scientists. Today, many women enjoy far more liberty than did their mothers and grandmothers. Unfortunately, this liberty and equality has not reached the vast majority of Indian women. A brief look at their current condition illustrates this point.

A snapshot of inequality

Illiteracy

Even after defining a literate -person to be anyone who can just sign his or her own name or write a simple sentence, according to the last census in 2001, only 54% of our women were literate as opposed to 75% of men.[2] This is considered to be a staggering gender gap. Of those women who are considered to be literate, 60% have just a primary school education or less.[2]

Our country offers "free and compulsory education for girls until the age of fourteen," and much progress has been made in this area. The difficult issue is keeping girls in school. Sometimes girls are withdrawn from school to fulfil family responsibilities: fetching water, collecting fuel wood and fodder, caring for siblings, cooking and cleaning. Girls tend to perform more chores than boys, so the benefit of keeping a daughter at home is greater. There is also the perception that educating a daughter will not benefit her parents. In addition, parents worry that if a daughter gets too educated it will be more difficult to find a match for her, because her husband will have to be better educated than her. A related concern for parents is that the more educated a man they have to find for their daughter, the higher the dowry expenses. Often girls are not allowed to attend school to protect their honour. Some parents are reluctant to allow their daughters to be taught by male teachers or to attend schools that are not separated by gender. The distance from home to school is also seen as a risk to a girl's safety.

Child Marriage

Almost half (47%) of our daughters are married before the legal age of 18.[3] There are many reasons cited for this: unmarried girls are unsafe; younger girls require less dowry; it is easier to find grooms for younger girls. In some regions, social pressure and old customs require girls to marry early and it is very difficult for any one parent to defy the system. In other areas, the severe shortage of girls is resulting in more and more child marriages.

Today, 40% of the world's child marriages occur in our country.[3]

Ill-health

Today, one woman dies in childbirth every five minutes.[4] This is a very high number by global standards: one-fifth of all maternal and child deaths during childbirth in the world occur in our country.[4] The high incidence of child marriage has a lot do to with this because maternal mortality is five times higher for girls under 15.[5] Poor access to health-care is another reason; less than half of all births in the country are supervised by health care professionals.[6]

Indian women are often the last to eat in their homes and often unlikely to eat well or rest during pregnancy. Almost 60% of pregnant women are anaemic.[6] Ill-health during pregnancy is compounded by illiteracy and ignorance, because a large percentage of pregnant women are extremely young teenagers. As a result, they give birth to low-weight babies and tend not to know how to feed them.

Almost half (48%) of our children under age five are stunted, an indicator of chronic malnutrition, and 70% of children under age five are anaemic.[6] Malnutrition makes children more prone to illness and stunts their physical and intellectual growth for a lifetime. If this child is a girl, she has the worst of it, because there is gender bias in feeding practices. Infant boys are fed more often and for longer periods of time. Medical attention, even basic preventative care like vaccinations, is often withheld from girls.

The issues of education, child marriage and health are intricately intertwined. For example, just a few years of schooling for the mother has been found to reduce the infant mortality rate by 40%.[7]

Financial Dependence

A vast majority of women work throughout their lives, in fact, many households would not survive without the income they bring in. Unfortunately however, much of a woman's work is "invisible" because it is not considered important by those around her and not recorded and acknowledged in the national workforce statistics. For example, most of the work women do – the collection of water, fuel and fodder (for which a woman may have to walk miles), cooking, cleaning, taking care of children and the elderly, and unpaid work on family land or in family enterprises – is completely invisible. Because they work at home, even the activities that contribute towards a living are considered part of domestic work. In his book, *Development as Freedom*, Nobel Laureate Dr Amartya Sen expresses this point very clearly:

> Men's relative dominance connects with a number of fac-tors, including the position of being the "breadwinner" whose economic power commands respect even within the family…While women work long hours every day at home, since this work does not produce a remuneration it is often ignored in the accounting of the respective contri-butions of women and men in the family's joint prosperity.
>
> *Dr Amartya Sen*

Many women are not allowed to join the workforce because it is perceived to diminish the family's status in society. When women do work because the family needs the income, they work both in the home and at a job outside the home, and their working hours are, in effect, double. In many homes, men's work and women's work is separate and clearly demarcated and men do not do women's work; it is perceived to be too demeaning.

In most industries, women are paid less than men for doing the same work. For example, the increased use of cheap female labour has become an important strategy for landowners to cut costs in agriculture. Employers say they prefer to use women because they are more industrious, work without breaks, and may be hired at 30% to 50% lower wages than men.[8]

Despite her tremendous and invaluable contributions, in most homes the woman herself does not have any control over the money she brings into the family; her father or husband controls it entirely. Where she does have control, statistics show that she invests more on the family and less on herself than her male counterpart, who tends to spend a larger proportion of his earnings on himself.

The great tragedy is that, in most families, women do not inherit anything from their parents. They do not own any property in their own names and do not get a share of parental property. Women own less than 1% of all the wealth in India.[9]

Social Conditioning

In our country, most women are materially, financially and socially dependent on men, and society offers them few alternatives. In most families, a woman is controlled by her father and brothers before marriage and by her husband and in-laws after marriage. She is conditioned from childhood to be docile, obedient and domestic. She is excluded from decision-making in every aspect of her life. Her objective in life is to cater to the comforts of the family – as a dutiful daughter, a loving mother, an obedient daughter-in-law and a faithful, submissive wife.

Gender bias restricts her mobility, education and acquisition of skills, ensuring she cannot earn an adequate income or ever become independent. Many women are not able to make the most basic of choices: whether and when to have a child. They are controlled to such an extent that they must take permission before they go to the market, or to visit friends and relatives.

Economic dependence makes women vulnerable to violence. Over 40% of Indian women face physical abuse by their husbands.[10] Violence against women in families is often justified as being necessary to "discipline" them and to punish them for dereliction of duty. What's worse is that women have come to accept this as their lot in life. Studies show that more than half of Indian women consider violence to be a normal part of married life and more than half of Indian women believe wife-beating to be justified in certain circumstances.[11]

Despite this, women would choose marriage over widowhood because many widows live deeply unhappy lives on the periphery of society. Often blamed for causing the death of their husbands by somehow bringing ill-luck, they are shunned at social functions and forced to live extremely restricted lives where everything they do – from what they wear to what they eat – is controlled.

This is not by any means a comprehensive snapshot of the inequality faced by women. They face many other issues, from AIDS to increased crime against women. In addition, all these issues are exacerbated when the woman is poor, and a large majority of women in our country live in extreme poverty.

Why is this happening? Why do we treat women like this? A step back into traditions, customs and mores reveals the answer.

Son-preference

India is in large part, and has been for a long period of history, a patriarchal society. We have always favoured our sons. Despite all the economic progress we have made, despite all the progressive education we have received, one thing has not changed: we have a deep-rooted tradition of son-preference.

Sons are an asset

In our society, sons are considered to be an asset for many reasons. First, sons continue the family lineage. If a family has only daughters it implies for many people the end of the *vansh*, the end of the family line. Also, unlike daughters, sons inherit and add to family wealth and property; this is crucial for those who have either property or a business to pass down and want to "keep it within the family."

> It is only a son that makes a father feel like a man and provides a stick in old age. We have so much of land. If I don't have a son, my brother-in-law's sons will get the lion's share.
>
> *Landowner in a village*[12]

Due to deep-rooted traditions, it is considered the son's duty to take care of his parents in their old age; most parents would not consider living with a daughter after she gets married and becomes "part of another family." There are other advantages to having a son. When parents die, convention dictates it is the son who lights the funeral pyre and performs particular rituals; there are many who believe they will not achieve salvation if they do not have a son to perform their last rites. In addition, there is a perception that sons defend the family and exercise family power; traditionally among the warrior castes, sons were a source of pride and strength, daughters were a source of vulnerability.

The desire for sons is not restricted to men alone. Women want sons too, and not just for the reasons mentioned. In our society, a woman's status increases when she gives birth to a son, increases further when her son reaches marriageable age and increases even further when she becomes a mother-in-law.

Daughters are a liability

Daughters are considered to be a liability and often an unbearable burden. Traditionally, daughters are believed to be *paraya dhan* – another's wealth. Many parents believe they feed, clothe and educate daughters only to have that "investment" completely taken over by the in-laws, because even if the girl is earning, her parents have no right to that earning. There is an oft-repeated saying that "bringing up a girl is like watering a neighbour's garden."

Perhaps the greatest challenge is that daughters are a huge financial burden, especially for the poor and middle classes, because of the crippling expense of marriage and dowry. Besides this, the cultural norms are such that daughters cannot be expected to take care of their parents in their old age. Another mark against them is that daughters have to be brought up with great care and caution due to the increasing lack of safety for women in our society. Daughters also have a lower earning potential compared to sons. And finally, the challenge of raising a daughter does not end after she gets married: very often a daughter is harassed and goes through great suffering at the hands of her husband and in-laws, further exacerbating her parents' pain and stress.

The combination of all these factors makes the birth of a daughter a painful event rather than a joyful one. The question we must ask ourselves is this: If our social norms dictate that a young girl's parents are not able to welcome her into the world with joy, what are the chances that society will subsequently allow her a life of dignity and respect?

Prabhuji mein tori binti karoon, paiyan paroon bar bar
Agle janam mohe bitiya na dije, narak dije chahe dar.
O God, I beg of you, I touch your feet time and again,
Next birth, don't give me a daughter, give me hell instead.

North Indian folk song

Dowry

Dowry is an Indian tradition that, far from serving any useful purpose, is poisoning our society. One would expect with increased education, economic growth and globalization, that the practice of dowry would die a natural death. Contrary to expectations, the practice has *increased substantially* in the past few decades. Initially dowry was something the rich indulged in; now it has penetrated deep into the lower income groups, creating a tremendous economic burden on families.

Many families in difficult financial circumstances feel harassed when a girl is born because they know the expense of getting her married and giving her a dowry will be financially crippling. The question of saying no to dowry does not arise. In most cases, refusal to offer a dowry will seal a girl's fate as a spinster and bring shame upon her family. What makes it worse is that dowry is not a one-time financial transaction; demands for dowry can go on for years after the marriage. Religious ceremonies and the birth of children often become occasions for further requests for money, cars or household articles. The inability of the bride's family to comply with these regular demands often leads to the daughter-in-law being subjected to the threat of divorce, abuse and, very often, severe torture.

There is a dowry death almost every hour in India!

More often than not, a girl's parents know she is being harassed or tortured but do not speak up or provide refuge, because society would ostracize them. In many cases, when the ill-treatment becomes unbearable a young woman will commit suicide to escape from it or to save her parents from further pain and financial ruin. In the worst cases "kitchen accidents" occur: wives are simply killed by the husband's family to make way for another marriage, which is, in effect, a new financial transaction.

Although dowry has been around for a while, it is India's recent materialism which has had a direct impact on this newer phenomenon of dowry-related crime. The first dowry death in India was reported in the mid-seventies. Today:

- A dowry-related death is reported once every 65 minutes.[13]
- Cruelty by husband and relatives is reported once every 7 minutes.[13]

These numbers are likely to be severe underestimates of the actual scale of dowry-related crime, most of which goes unreported. Most women suffer in silence for many reasons: they have children at home; they are financially dependent on their husbands; shelters are often unbearable choices where hygienic conditions are below par and vulnerable women are further exploited; law enforcement is apathetic; parents are not supportive; and society would blame and shun them if they left their husbands.

A lethal combination: son-preference, dowry and India's new materialism

Although son-preference and dowry are old traditions, they are bumping up against the new India – fast-paced, materialistic, acquisitive and technologically savvy – and taking on a new shape. In the new India, modern conveniences and wealthy lifestyles are advertised daily on TV. Those who aspire for this "good life" see dowry as a means to effortlessly escape poverty, increase family wealth, or acquire modern conveniences. Also, in this new India, status is of increasing importance. Given this scenario, sons are crucial: sons earn more; sons can demand dowry and thus bring in even more; sons can inherit and keep family possessions within the family; and sons can go abroad for work, further enhancing the parents' status. As a result, parents are desperate for sons.

To be the parents of a son is an empowering experience. To be the parents of a daughter can be a shattering experience.

Son-preference and dowry are serious social ills with grave consequences for our daughters. Unfortunately, instead of fighting these social evils we are trying to solve the problem by getting rid of the girl-child. *The thinking is: if there is no daughter, there will be no problem.*

Sex-selection

The practice of killing baby girls after they are born, female infanticide, has existed in India for centuries.

> "In Punjab, Haryana and Rajasthan, the practice of killing new-born girls is part of our history. When a girl was born, the head of the family would place a ball of cotton in one hand and a piece of jaggery in her other hand, and say to her, *'Pooni katin te gud khayin, veeru nu bhejin, aap na aayin.'* (Spin the cotton and eat the sweet; next time don't come yourself, send your brother instead). The baby girl was then placed in an earthen pot and the mouth of the pot sealed. The *dayi* (midwife) was sent to abandon the pot in some deserted place. This was an accepted practice in society; it was viewed neither as a sin nor as an unlawful act."

Dr Keerti Kesar as related to Vikas Sharma
"Waqt Badal Dega Tasveer"
Dainik Bhaskar, 22 October, 2009

Contrary to what one might expect, this practice has *increased substantially* in recent decades.

> "...When a male child is born, women bang *thalis* (metal plates) or fire in the air to announce his birth. But if a girl is born, an elderly woman of the house goes and asks the male members, *'baraat rakhni hai ya lautani?'* (Do you want to welcome the marriage procession or shall we bid them to return?) If the reply is *'lautani hai'* (to return), everyone leaves and the mother is asked to put tobacco into the girl's mouth. There is no question of resistance, as it would mean that the mother herself is at risk of either being killed or thrown out of the house."
>
> *Personal communication during fieldwork,*
> *45 Million Daughters Missing*[14]

With the advent of more advanced technologies, the practice of infanticide has transformed itself into the less overt and far more prevalent practice of female foeticide. Technology now makes it possible to detect the sex of the child in the womb, and many parents, once they find out it is a girl, choose to abort the foetus.

What is the scale of sex-selection in our country?

The scale of sex-selection is estimated using an indicator called *Sex Ratio*: the ratio of females per 1000 males. In most countries women exceed men, because women tend to outlive men: in 2008, Japan had 1053 women to a 1000 men and the United States had 1027 women to a 1000 men. India's estimated sex ratio for the same year is very low: 936 women to a 1000 men.

Child Sex Ratio, a more accurate indicator of sex-selection and girl-child neglect, is the ratio of girl children per 1000 boy children in the age group of 0–6 years. The Child Sex Ratio in the census of 2001 was 927 girls to 1000 boys.

It is estimated that over 50 million women are missing from our population today, and this is largely attributed to the practice of sex-selection. A UNFPA report estimates that in 1991, up to 48 million women were missing from India's population. The report hypothesizes that if the sex ratio in Kerala in 1991 had prevailed in the whole country, India would have had 48 million more women.[15] If this is an estimate of the number of women missing from the population in 1991, the current number is surely far in excess of that.

Over 50 million women are missing in India today!

One would imagine it must be the most rural, poor and illiterate families who are killing their daughters. However, the opposite is true.

Urban India is doing it more than rural India
The sex ratio is far worse in urban India than in rural India. There are some urban communities with as few as 300 girls per 1000 boys, and it is India's major metropolises that have some of the poorest sex ratios.

The rich are doing it more than the poor
Again, contrary to expectations, the rich and the middle-class are eliminating daughters at a faster rate than the poor. For the poor, the motivation to abort a daughter is the fear of having to pay dowry at a later date. Affluent families can afford the dowry,

but they have either a business or property to pass down, and as a result are obsessed with the idea of having sons.

The literate are doing it more than the illiterate

One might expect that increased education would solve the problem, but educated families are sex-selecting more than illiterate families. Urban, educated and prosperous parents tend to have smaller families, have knowledge of the latest technology, and can more easily afford the expenses of ultrasounds and abortions. As a result, an increasing number of families are using technology to "balance" their families.

The PC & PNDT Act was enacted in 1994, and amended in 2003, making sex-selection an illegal, criminal act in India. But law enforcement has not been effective in stemming the tide of this horrific form of gender discrimination.

More details are provided in the last chapter of the book, "A Final Note," which includes statistics and information about the scale of sex-selection, the uphill battle against it, and the experiences of women who live through it every day.

The systematic elimination
of daughters from our society
has reached such crisis proportions
that some people have called it
a "holocaust" and a "silent genocide."

3

THE CONSEQUENCES
OF OUR ACTIONS

> *As long as the birth of a girl does not*
> *receive the same welcome as that of a*
> *boy, so long we should know that India*
> *is suffering from partial paralysis.*
> Mahatma Gandhi

Today, India *is* suffering from this partial paralysis. How can there be widespread cruelty, neglect and inequality without some tragic consequence? And what is the impact of inequality and unabated sex-selection on our society?

Impact on women

"Sau putravati bhava" (May you be the mother of a hundred sons)…This is a well-known blessing given to a young girl when she gets married. In our country, there is tremendous pressure on women to bear sons, to the extent that they are made to feel like failures if they do not. Often they are threatened with abandonment and divorce if they do not eliminate a baby girl.

The desire of every woman is to be the mother of at least one son. A childless woman is an "incomplete" woman and one who only has daughters is also only partially complete. It is only after she has produced a son that she enjoys a status of sorts.

One person voicing the prevailing
opinion in their community[12]

The physical health of these women is at serious risk. Studies indicate that the risk of death is seven to ten times higher for women who wait until the second trimester to terminate their pregnancies; sex-selective abortions are all second trimester abortions. There is evidence of women undergoing as many as eight consecutive abortions to fulfil the family's quest for a son. A large percentage of Indian women are anaemic and consecutive abortions ruin their health. Many women go through tremendous physical suffering and psychological trauma as a result of forcibly undergoing abortion after abortion. Many poor women contract disease, get bed-ridden or die due to ill-performed abortions in unhygienic conditions like mobile vans.

Women have nothing to do with the gender of the baby

The sex chromosomes in men and women are different. There are two kinds of sex chromosomes: 'X' and 'Y'. Modern science tells us that during fertilization, the woman always contributes an 'X' chromosome. If the man contributes an 'X' chromosome the baby will be a girl. If the man contributes a 'Y' chromosome, the baby will be a boy.

Therefore, it is *only* the sex chromosome of the man which determines the gender of the baby.

Impact on children

The children of today are tomorrow's future generation. A mother is a child's first teacher and a very strong influence in the child's life. What joy can a mother bring into her child's life when she is unhappy in her marriage due to constant dowry demands or incessant pressure to bear a son? What values are we imparting to vulnerable, impressionable children who grow up in a home where the mother is constantly dominated and abused? What behaviour will these children exhibit when they grow up?

Impact on men

Today, due to sex-selection, there is a severe shortage of women in some communities. Men who are not able to find a bride due to this shortage of women will be deprived of one of the great joys of life: experiencing a wife's life-long companionship and support.

Also, ours is a society where marriage is regarded as universally desirable. Social status and acceptance depend, in large part, on being married and creating a new family. Men who are not able to find a bride will experience the pain and loneliness of being marginalized by society.

Increased crime in society

The supporters of sex-detection tests argue that on the basis of the law of demand and supply, an excess of males over females would eventually *raise* the status of women.

> Whatever is happening should be allowed to continue unchecked. The value of women will shoot up and they will come on horseback and take the boys away.
>
> *The opinion of one doctor arguing*
> *to allow sex-selective abortions*[12]

History proves, on the other hand, that an adverse sex ratio in a society results in increased violence against women. This has already begun to occur in India. The shortage of women in certain areas has resulted in a marked increase in crime in those areas. The following crimes were committed against women in 2007:[13]

- 1 woman was sexually harassed every 48 minutes
- 1 woman or minor girl was abducted every 26 minutes
- 1 woman was raped every 25 minutes
- 1 woman was molested every 14 minutes

These numbers are based on reported crimes. The vast majority of crimes against women in our country go unreported.

UNICEF recently concluded that "the alarming decline in the child sex ratio [in India] is likely to result in more girls being married at a younger age, more girls dropping out of education, increased mortality as a result of early child-bearing and associated increase in acts of violence against girls and women such as rape, abduction, trafficking and forced polyandry."[16]

Bride-buying and polyandry

Bride-buying and polyandry are relatively new "crimes" against women and are directly related to sex-selection. In parts of India where the shortage of women is acute, there is an increasing trend towards buying brides from poorer regions or from lower castes. "Brokers" are used to traffic women, creating a thriving business. Many of these bought women have no proper registration of their marriage, which makes them vulnerable to exploitation by their husband's male relatives and friends. Often the woman is forced to be "wife" not only to her husband, but also to his brothers. There are instances of women who are married to as many as eight brothers within the same family. Known as *draupadis*, these women inhabit the very lowest rungs of the family and societal hierarchy and are subjected to ongoing physical and sexual abuse.

Increased social instability and unrest

In many communities in India today, there are growing numbers of young men in the lower echelons of society who are marginalized because of their inability to find a wife and who have little outlet for their sexual energy. There is evidence that when such single young men congregate, the potential for organized aggression is likely to increase substantially. Experts predict that this situation will lead to increased levels of anti-social behaviour and violence and will ultimately present a threat to the stability and security of society.[17]

Is this the society we want to live in?
Is this the society we want
to pass on to our children?
Perhaps we should pause
and reflect on the traditions
which drive our choices.

4

WHAT CHOICES
ARE WE MAKING?

> *When there is oppression, the only*
> *self-respecting thing is to rise and*
> *say this shall cease today, because*
> *my right is justice.*
>
> Sarojini Naidu

Perhaps we are shocked by the facts presented in this book. We should be! When viewed comprehensively, the facts about the escalation and consequences of sex-selection are shocking enough to make us feel very disturbed. So let us ask ourselves some questions about the choices that are implicit to these statistics.

What choices are we making as a society?

Are we a nation of mass murderers? Whose job is it to protect our daughters? Does a girl not have a right to be born in our country?

For how long can we continue to tolerate or justify the cruelties perpetrated on women as somehow required by tradition?

How is our society well-served by a tradition that forces a woman to practically sever her relationship with her parents when she gets married; that denies her the right to take care of her elderly parents; that denies her an inheritance from her parents? How is our society well-served when our Constitution is set aside, and half our population is denied the same rights to education, health, freedom, opportunity and equality as the other half?

What place does a tradition like dowry have in the 21st century? Why do we even accept as normal such a one-sided, oppressive practice? Is it not time to relegate the ancient tradition of dowry into the trash bin of history, right along with other such traditions like *sati*?

After parents have killed off their daughters, where will they go to find brides for their sons? Can our society afford to have hundreds of thousands of unmarried, marginalized men with no outlet for their frustration? Are we comfortable with the rate at which crime against women is steadily increasing? Are we comfortable with the prospect of practices like bride-buying and polyandry becoming so commonplace that they become the traditions of our future?

When we read about a dowry death or female foeticide in the newspaper and just turn the page, unaffected, is it because we have become hard-hearted and indifferent, or has our own sense of powerlessness made us numb? And if *we* do not react to this outrage, who will?

How many people are trapped in their everyday habits: part numb, part frightened, part indifferent? To have a better life we must keep choosing how we are living.

Albert Einstein

What choices are we making as a family?

As a nation, we pride ourselves on our strong family values. Let us reflect on this for a moment...What are these family values? Is it a family value to love our sons but not our daughters; to love our sons but not our daughters-in-law; to marry off a vulnerable, under-aged child; to sell our daughters in the dowry market; to disinherit our daughters? Is it a family value to artificially "balance" the family – to have a son by killing preceding daughters?

Surely our values are, instead, to create a family in which all members are loved and treated equally, where all members are empowered to make decisions, and where all are given equal opportunity to achieve their utmost. Surely we realize that the way we treat any one relationship in the family will eventually affect every other relationship in the family.

> If we do not teach our children, society will.
> And they – and we – will live with the results.
>
> *Stephen Covey*

Marriage is one of the key institutions of civilization. For a marriage to be successful, it takes two people, a man and a woman, working in partnership. The family unit they create is a fundamental building block of society, the medium through which we impart values to the next generation. When there is no emotional stability in the family unit, it is traumatic for children. Unstable and unhappy children will go on to create an unstable and chaotic society. On the other hand, a happy family with strong family values will produce children with high self-esteem, children who enrich the world around them, children who are catalysts of change.

What choices are we making as individuals?

Do we believe God makes a mistake when he gives us a baby girl? Do we realize that we are trying to "play God" when we tamper with the natural order of things?

Modern technology will keep moving forward; it cannot be stopped. But technology is in the hands of human beings – it is in *our* hands – and we have to individually exercise our discrimination when we use it. Nuclear technology was a great invention, but it can be used to provide energy to millions of people or to kill millions in an instant. The choice is ours. Ultrasound technology was meant to detect diseases in the foetus and to protect both mother and baby from harm. Now it is being misused as a tool for sex-selection. Again, the choice is ours.

Today, sex-selective abortion is considered to be wrong because it involves taking a life. But this may not always be the case. Pre-implantation genetic techniques are being developed that will make it possible to *pre-determine* the sex of the child. When this technology becomes readily available we will be able to have a son without the mess and guilt of an abortion. Will such gender determination be a moral act? It will still be sex-selection. Is it for us to choose the gender of our children? One day, we may be able to choose to have a son who is perfect – 6 feet tall, with beautiful features and great strength and intellect. Will we then choose this option? Where will the quest for a perfect son end?

Things which matter most must never be at the mercy of things which matter least.

Goethe

Is the thing which matters most – our own soul – at the mercy of things that will, at the end of our days, not matter in the least: worldly riches, family name and status in society? As we try to increase our wealth and status – by having sons at the expense of daughters, taking dowry and hosting lavish weddings – are we not compromising on our principles in the process? Can a life built on another's suffering ever bring us happiness?

Are we comfortable with the choices
we are making – as individuals,
as families, as a society?
Indifference is also an action.
Silence is also a choice.
If each one of us does not
do something to stem this crisis,
we will have to face
the consequences of our silence.

5

THE SPIRITUAL PERSPECTIVE

> *For what is a man profited, if he shall*
> *gain the whole world, and lose his*
> *own soul?*
>
> Matthew 16:26

We have seen how invaluable women are to the natural order; we have seen their current condition; and we have seen the social consequences of our actions toward them. The spiritual consequences of our actions, on the other hand, are far more subtle. Saints and great visionaries of every religion, in every age, have given us essentially the same unequivocal message again and again. What, we can ask ourselves, would be their perspective on this grave crisis?

Upsetting the balance in nature

There has always been a balance in nature. This natural, God-given balance in the universe comes from pairs of opposites complementing each other. Light and dark, day and night, young and old, aggressive and passive, masculine and feminine, man and woman – all are important to this balance and well-being of the creation. Human beings have both masculine and feminine characteristics, and men and women together contribute to a balanced society.

> Why did God make some of us men and others women? Because a woman's love is one image of the love of God, and a man's love is another image of God's love. Both are created to love, but each in a different way.
>
> *Mother Teresa*

Today, the massive scale of sex-selection threatens the male-female balance in our society. The absence of one gender, the female, upsets the natural balance. An excess of masculine energy without the gentling, harmonizing influence of the feminine to complement it, leads to chaos and destruction.

It is not our job to try to create the "perfect family;" it is not our job to "balance" the family. Nature balances itself. When we interfere with the processes of nature, we disrupt the natural order of things. Then nature asserts itself to correct the imbalance. This process of correction is inevitably a painful one.

Aligning our actions with our goals

What is our life's ultimate goal? If our goal is spiritual, then let us ask ourselves, are our daily actions aligned with this goal? Many of us tend to fall into the trap of limiting our spiritual efforts to a particular time or place: We perform a few moments of ritual at a place of worship or a few moments of prayer at a particular time every day, and then for the rest of the day we forget our noble goal. At times we may even perform acts of such callousness toward our fellow human beings that every act of worship we have performed might stand cancelled. Is such worship acceptable to the Lord?

> In the court of the Lord, an ounce of love
> Weighs more than tons of religious faith.
>
> *Hazrat Sultan Bahu, BAIT 58*

To achieve the highest spiritual goal, we have to *live* the spiritual teachings at every moment. The spiritual way must become an inherent part of our lives.

The essential equality of women

Saints teach us about the sacred nature and oneness of all living beings.

> From one Light all have emanated, then who can we call good and who bad?
>
> *Kabir Sahib*

Our soul, the life force that enables us to live, has no gender. In the eyes of God there is no difference between men and women: all are pure spirit, all are divine, all are equal.

Taking a life

Saints have always maintained that every life has value, that it is wrong to kill another being. They teach us only God has the power to give life and take life: it is not for us to decide on God's behalf whom to preserve and whom to kill.

> Thou shalt not kill.
>
> *Ten Commandments of the Bible*
> *as quoted in Matthew 5:21*

> You shall not kill your children due to fear of poverty. We provide for them, as well as for you. Killing them is a gross offence.
>
> *Qur'an [17:31]*

> Do not kill any creature;
>   in all beings dwells the Lord.
> O Ravidas, the sin of killing will not be atoned for,
> Even if one were to give a million cows in charity.
>
> *Guru Ravidas*

Perhaps we are confused because we see the child in question as an unborn foetus, not a living baby. Infanticide, though still widely practised, has always been associated with guilt: the mother has a chance to hold her baby in her arms; the *dayi* (midwife) who usually performs the act, has a chance to see the face of the baby and hears her cry and struggle for life. In the old days, after killing a girl-child, a *pundit* was called to the house to perform prayers and make offerings to appease the gods. We have always known, deep down inside, that it is wrong.

Unfortunately with foeticide, because the baby is unborn and unseen, our conscience is relatively numb. Medical technology, the clinic and the professionalism of the medical team distance us from the cruelty of the act. Also, many of us find foeticide morally acceptable because we believe the soul does not enter the foetus until the end of the second trimester of gestation. We must ask ourselves: on what basis have we reached this conclusion?

Nature intended the mother's womb to be a safe place for the baby to grow. A foetus has the ability to experience pain; a foetus is a human being in the making – the greatest of all God's creations. A foetus is a human child born in the image of God; a child brings the promise of love. It is our responsibility to protect and nurture that innocent child as much and as far as we can.

Hurting another human being

When we view all beings through a spiritual lens, it creates compassion in us. We begin to understand that far from killing, we should not even injure another's feelings. Daughter, sister, wife, daughter-in-law – we cannot expect to hurt her and find a place for ourselves in the court of the Lord.

> Never hurt the feelings of anyone. This is a sin which even God himself does not pardon, because it cuts at the very root of spirituality.
>
> *Maharaj Jagat Singh*

Putting limits on our wants

Let us pause and reflect on our motivations. What is it that makes us demand a dowry? And even if we have not asked for a dowry, what makes us accept these gifts when they are given, as if it were our birthright to take, and their fate to give?

Do our expectations and desires exceed our needs? To what extent are we willing to go for a better TV, a newer car, a bigger house? And if all these desires were to be fulfilled, would we then be satisfied, or would our mind conjure up new wants?

> We should remain, then, within the limits imposed by our basic needs and strive with all our power not to exceed them. For once we are carried a little beyond these limits in our desire for the pleasures of this life, there is then no criterion by which to check the onward movement, since no bounds can be set to that which exceeds the necessary.
>
> *Philokalia*

In our need to possess more, have we given any thought to the repercussions that will surely follow?

> You clutch at things that belong to another,
> But the Lord within knows and hears all.
> Lost in greed for worldly things,
> You fall into the pit of hell,
> Unaware of what lies in store for you in the beyond.
>
> *Guru Arjun Dev*

The desire for sons and the desire for more wealth lead us to commit heinous acts against women. But do either our sons or our wealth truly belong to us? Will we be able to take them with us when we leave this world?

> The fool is tormented, thinking,
> "These sons belong to me,"
> "This wealth belongs to me."

He himself does not belong to himself.
How then can sons be his?
How then can wealth be his?

Dhammapada

The consequences of our actions

The law of karma is a natural law that governs the working of this creation. According to this law of cause and effect, our every thought and action results in an equivalent consequence.

Whatever we sow, it is that we shall reap; this life is a field of actions.

Guru Arjun Dev

A record is kept by life itself of all our thoughts and actions. We may have to bear the consequence of these actions in this lifetime, or it may be postponed to a future lifetime. Either way, the consequence itself is inescapable. There is an apt saying: the wheels of karma grind slow, but they grind exceedingly fine.

A story in the Indian epic, the *Mahabharata*, illustrates the working of this law quite effectively. The king Dhritarashtra was born blind and he considered this fate a terrible curse. Due to great good karma, however, he was granted the spiritual power to be able to see his past lives. He looked back one hundred lives searching for some clue that would indicate why he had been cursed with blindness in this life, but he could find no action he'd done to warrant his fate. He turned to Lord Krishna, who advised him to look back beyond a hundred lives. When he did, he discovered that in one particular lifetime, as a young "ignorant" child, he had poked thorns into the eyes of some helpless animal. Due to this act he was now, many lifetimes later, born as a blind king.

> O friend, the record of thy deeds cannot be effaced;
> They are recorded by (the law of) God.
>
> *Guru Nanak*

Sometimes, after committing what we know to be a wrong act, we may feel complacent because we were able to escape the law of the land. Hazur Maharaj Charan Singh used to say that if a five-year-old child were in the same room with us, we would hesitate to steal even a pencil. Yet what do we not do in the presence of the Lord? We should be cautioned: the Lord who is all-knowing and all-seeing cannot be deceived.

> Be not deceived; God is not mocked;
> For whatsoever a man soweth, that shall he also reap.
>
> *Bible, Galatians 6:7–6:9*

Nor should we be beguiled into thinking that our actions are somehow justified because our circumstances are desperate or because we are doing this for our loved ones. On our Day of Judgment it is we who will be held accountable for our actions, not our loved ones. No one else can pay this debt for us.

> Each soul earns what it earns for itself; and no man shall bear another's burden.
>
> *Qur'an*

It is a sin to kill. Nothing in this world is free; everything we do comes at a price. We may have the sons, we may have the wealth, but we had to sell our soul in exchange for it: was it worth the price? Will we ever again be able to live in peace?

Living in the will of the Lord

To accept the will of the Lord means to understand that the events in our life are not occurring arbitrarily. We made choices in our past lives and we are reaping the fruits of those actions. Therefore, if a daughter is in our destiny, then so be it; let us welcome her with equal love. Her presence in her mother's womb is not an accident to be corrected, but an act of supreme will.

> Not a leaf can stir without his command.
>
> *Punjabi proverb as quoted by Maharaj Charan Singh*

Why can we not accept the Lord's will? What are we worried about? Continuing the family lineage? Keeping the inheritance within the family? Having financial and emotional support in our old age? Meeting our business and financial goals? Let us set aside these worries; let us just do what is right and turn to the Lord to take care of us in our time of need.

> Your worrying shows that you have no faith in the goodness of God or even in God himself. Let him accomplish things in his own way rather than in the way you desire. Try to adjust yourself to all that he does and you will never be unhappy.
>
> *Maharaj Jagat Singh*

And if God cares so wonderfully for flowers that are here today and gone tomorrow, won't he more surely care for you? You have so little faith!

Luke 12:23

If we look at our relationships and possessions from a spiritualized perspective we will realize that, in truth, everything we have does not belong to us. What we have has been entrusted to our care for a time, so let us not cling to it, compromise our principles, or try to impose our will over the Lord's. As caretakers our job is to take ourselves out of our actions and just discharge our duty with the utmost sincerity, honesty and love, and leave the results in the Lord's hands.

If we can take what comes to us as from Him, then whatever it is becomes divine itself; shame becomes honour, bitterness becomes sweet, and darkness becomes light. Everything takes its flavour from God and becomes divine. Everything that happens betrays the invisible hand of God.

Maharaj Charan Singh

Our essential divinity

Let us ask ourselves an important question. Who are we? We think of ourselves as human beings struggling to survive, occasionally searching for meaning through an elusive spiritual experience. Saints, however, offer us a far broader perspective:

We are not human beings having a spiritual experience.
We are spiritual beings having a human experience.

Pierre Teilhard de Chardin

What a paradigm shift this is! Do we really see ourselves as spiritual beings? This is a question of fundamental importance because our self-perception is the lens through which we view the world and the driver of all our actions towards others. It is only when we respect ourselves that we are able to treat others with respect. It is only when we love ourselves that we can have any love to give to others. It is only when we consider ourselves to be divine that we see the divinity in others.

Our actions towards others are, in fact, a mirror which reflects how we view ourselves.

We cannot ignore this fundamental fact:
To kill a child is a sin. To hurt a woman –
by thoughts, words or actions – is a sin.
When we hurt, abuse, or dominate
anyone in our lives we will have to bear
the consequences of our actions.
Any pain perpetrated by us will stand in the way
of our own spiritual progress and growth.
Let us, instead, wake up
to our great human potential.
Let us live a life that gives equal value
to each human being
no matter whether they are
woman or man, girl child or boy child.
We are all born of one sacred reality.

6

OLD TRADITIONS
CAN BE BROKEN

> *Everything can be taken from a person*
> *but one thing: the last of human*
> *freedoms – to choose one's attitude*
> *in any given set of circumstances, to*
> *choose one's own way.*
>
> Viktor Frankl

Who is responsible for the suffering of our women? And what is the solution?

Why do women hurt women?

Although the impression given is that women are oppressed by men, this is not always the case. As people are quick to point out there are many cases where *women* are the instigators or perpetrators. Why do women, who have themselves faced inequality and oppression, turn around and hurt other women? Let us examine several scenarios which we see occurring in the lives of women every day.

Why does a poor, uneducated woman willingly choose to eliminate her fourth daughter? Perhaps because all her other "choices" have been taken away from her: her husband refuses to take contraception and does not allow her to either; she cannot afford to bring up another child; she cannot afford another dowry; she has "had it" – had enough with the incessant cycle of childbirth, nursing and rearing over which she has no control; she is physically exhausted after years of bearing the double burden of working outside the home and taking care of her family. In her mind, an abortion is the only choice she has.

Choice in the absence of autonomy is no choice at all.

Why does a wealthy, educated woman choose to abort her daughter? Unfortunately neither wealth nor education necessarily equate with high self-esteem. Perhaps this woman has been brainwashed from childhood to accept the "reality" that sons are necessary to carry on the family line and inherit the wealth. Perhaps this woman does not have the self-esteem required to resist pressure from her husband and his family to "keep trying till we have a son."

Young women are not born with high self-esteem. Self-respect, self-confidence and self-esteem are precious gifts which her parents and society have the power to either give to her or withhold from her.

Why do some mothers-in-law oppress their daughters-in-law?

Preeta Mehta (name changed), age 31 years: Ever since the birth of her daughter, her mother-in-law hasn't stopped berating her, pointing out that all her husband's cousins have sons. The mother-in-law insists that to perpetuate the family name, she too must have a son. "She tells me to have an abortion if I conceive a girl," she says. Her husband agrees with his mother. What does she herself want? "I don't know."

Shefalee Vasudev, "Missing Girl-Child"

Women hurt women for the same reason that prisoners exploit other prisoners, and beggar children bully other beggar children on the street. It is our human nature that if we are needy and can do anything to get a little more – an extra *roti*, a few rupees, a little more status, power or leisure – we will do it. Within a family, if all the women are economically and socially dependent on the same male – whether the head of the household is a father, a brother or a son – and they all have to compete with each other for security, recognition, attention and love, this situation may naturally make them into each other's enemies.

Besides, brain-washing and social conditioning are very powerful forces. In a patriarchal society women are victims of tremendous social pressure to toe the line. In the days of *sati*, who was it who shaped a girl's thinking from childhood to accept the "reality" that to become a *sati* was her ultimate destiny? It was her own mother. Who dressed the young widow as a bride and led her to the funeral pyre to be burnt alive with her husband? It was the women around her, and they did it knowing that one day this could be their own destiny. Women hurt women because they have been conditioned to accept their own inferiority from their very infancy. This is what makes patriarchy work – gaining a woman's complicity in her own inequality.

When a bird has been kept in a cage from its infancy and then many years later the cage door is opened, what are the chances the bird will take the opportunity to fly? She may hop out, but then will hop back into her comfort zone, even if that means being imprisoned all her life. For such a bird, the prospect of soaring is not liberating, it is frightening.

This is exactly how we have crippled so many of our women. Perhaps instead of judging them, we can find it in our hearts to have compassion for them, or at the very least, understanding. For they are victims of the system as much the women they victimize.

Who is responsible for this crisis?

When we hear about the great injustices perpetrated on women, perhaps our first reaction is to apportion blame. Who is responsible, we want to know? What are the law enforcement agencies doing? The answer to the question – who is responsible? – is not what we might expect.

To begin with, there are very few women in law enforcement. Moreover, law enforcement – the police force and the judiciary – consists of people who are drawn from society; they have the same beliefs as the rest of us. There have been numerous occasions when a policeman has turned away a hapless woman who has come to file a complaint about dowry torture, telling her kindly that a woman's place is with her husband; telling her she should try to reconcile her differences with him.

One study conducted to assess the attitudes of judges towards violence against women found that *a very large percentage of judges believed that there were certain occasions when it was justifiable for a husband to slap his wife; that the preservation of the family should be a woman's primary concern even if she faces violence; that "provocative" clothes are an invitation to sexual assault; and that dowry has an inherent cultural value.*[18] These beliefs are deep-rooted in our society.

Law enforcement blames parents for the dowry system: when parents themselves give and take dowry freely, they say, it is very hard to enforce the law. And law enforcement blames both parents and doctors for the crisis caused by sex-selection: it is not easy to enforce the law, they say, when the decision to abort a girl is freely made by her parents and the doctor in a closed room in a medical clinic.

Doctors, in turn, blame the parents who come to them with the request. Many doctors believe they are fulfilling a social need; they believe that if they did not perform the abortion the parents would get it done from some other doctor anyway; and they believe that the life of the girl, if she were allowed to live, would be miserable. Many doctors believe they are being merciful to both the parents and the unborn daughter by fulfilling the parents' wish to abort her.

> How can you deny her [the mother] the right to have a son instead of a third or fourth daughter? You can't wish away centuries of thinking by saying that boys and girls are equal...it is better to get rid of an unwanted child than to make it suffer all its life.
>
> *The opinion of one doctor*[19]

Parents turn around and blame society. They say societal norms, traditions and pressures have put them in such an untenable situation that they have no option but to get rid of their daughters.

And so we come full circle. The answer to the question – who is responsible? – is not pleasant. *We,* the society, are responsible. When we point one finger, there are three pointing back at us. We are the parents, neighbours, doctors, policemen and judges who must change our values. We are the teachers who must teach our children about equality between the sexes. We are the politicians and administrators who must implement the laws. We are the members of the media who must raise public awareness and bring about change.

We are all responsible.

What is the solution?

Since we are all part of the problem, we must all be part of the solution. The solution lies in the choices we make – as individuals and as a society.

Human beings have a God-given gift, a quality called *vivek*, or discrimination: the ability to distinguish right action from wrong. Let us use this sense of discrimination to choose right actions. Let us choose to be contented, compassionate, law-abiding and loving human beings.

To make moral choices, we may have to forsake some of our traditions. Undoubtedly, this will not be easy. Our traditions and beliefs are so deep-rooted, we tend to carry them with us even when we emigrate to a different country. Today, female foeticide is prevalent in the Indian community in Western countries like the USA, Canada and the UK. And NRI Indians who come back to India to find brides command the highest rates in the dowry market.

It is hard to give up old traditions because we are proud of them. Our customs are rooted in an ancient heritage that goes back centuries. Traditions create a comfort zone: a known, familiar set of behaviours passed down by our parents and grandparents which generate a sense of security. And traditions serve a purpose: they create stability in society.

However, as a society matures and develops, old traditions give way to new. To stay healthy and in step with the times the culture adapts. Our country's strength over the centuries has been its capability to adapt and absorb new forces, new knowledge, new thought. India's rich and extraordinary cultural heritage is because of this. And just imagine: if we had not demonstrated the ability to give up old traditions and old ways of thinking, a woman would not be allowed to vote; she would not be educated; she would certainly not be allowed to remarry – she would probably be placed on the funeral pyre with her dead husband and burnt alive with him.

These were all traditions at one time, yet we have moved beyond them. We were able to do this because we knew in our heart that blind adherence to old, irrelevant traditions would poison and weaken our society. And we were able to do this because there were some courageous people in our society at the time who were catalysts of change.

So, where does change begin?

It is probably true to say that the largest scope for change still lies in men's attitude towards women, and in women's attitude towards themselves.

Vera Brittain

Changing women's attitude towards themselves

The most fundamental change in thinking must begin in the minds of women themselves.

Today a woman's attitudes and her entire belief system are controlled by the social customs of the past. Her self-esteem is developed from the meaning that others give her. Her self-esteem depends on her ability to successfully carry out the limited roles that her community has given her. Women often lack the self-confidence and belief in their own ability to take on further roles that will emancipate them.

But the truth is that every woman holds extraordinary power within herself. She is special. She must reach beyond her inhibitions and fears to fulfil her dreams with courage and determination. And she must do this both for her own sake and for the sake of her family.

Every woman is a role model for her daughter. A woman with high self-esteem will teach her daughter to esteem and value herself. A woman who pursues her dream will free her daughter to fly.

Changing men's attitude towards women

Resistance to change is natural because old beliefs and attitudes have been ingrained in us for generations. Our mindsets are deep-rooted. They are hard to tear up from their soil. It will take great courage on the part of men to give up positions of power which have always been their domain and right. It will take great courage to move out of their comfort zone. But real change will only occur when a man's thinking undergoes a transformation. Men must understand that empowering women will not pose a threat to them or disrupt harmony in the family and community. Rather it will enhance life, not just for them but for the entire family.

Today men have the power to raise or lower the status of the women in their lives. A woman's status at home will largely determine her standing in the world. Respect for a woman, for her needs and aspirations, is essential, because only then will she give her best to her home and society. A happy woman will make a loving home and bring up sons and daughters who have a healthy outlook towards life.

Every man is a role model for his son. Children listen not to our words, but rather they learn from our behaviour. When a man has the courage to treat his wife with dignity and respect he teaches his son to treat *all* women with dignity and respect.

Becoming catalysts of change

There are several examples of courage from different parts of India where individual people are breaking with old traditions and allowing their conscience to speak up against the prevailing norm.

Kanya Lohri in Sheopur Kassi...

One example of change is the small village of Sheopur Kassi in Sri Gangananagar, a district with the lowest sex ratio in Rajasthan. The people of the village could see that the male-female imbalance would have far-reaching repercussions and they decided to do something about it. They celebrated a *Kanya Lohri* festival and honoured 101 baby girls in front of a 7000-strong crowd. This is especially significant because traditionally *Lohri* is a festival in which sweets are offered in a large bonfire to seek blessings for the longevity and good health of male infants. In the same village two young girls performed the last rites for their mother, breaking the age-old tradition of sons performing the last rites for parents.[20]

A baarat comes to a village after 115 years...

Deora was a village in which for six generations and more than 100 years, no girl-child was allowed to live. Female infanticide was a tradition there. Babies were killed soon after birth in the labour room itself. It was an open secret. Everyone knew, everyone tacitly approved. If outsiders asked for a reason the villagers would say that the water in the well was such that only sons were born there. All this stopped when Indra Singh and his wife said "no more." A daughter had been born to them just fifteen days after a son had died, and he and his wife could not bring themselves to kill her. They literally gave their daughter, Jaswant Kanwar, the gift of life.

Young Jaswant was an oddity in the village initially, but her father, who went on to become *sarpanch* (village headman), educated her until the eighth grade which is as far as the village school could educate any child, boy or girl. Emboldened by Indra Singh's decision, his brother and uncle both had a daughter each. Jaswant Kanwar was married in 1998. People from all over the region came to witness the occasion. The last time the village had seen a girl's marriage was in 1883. Today, although infanticide still occurs, it is possible to see young girls in the village. Indra Singh and his wife had the courage to break an unquestioned tradition. They were catalysts of change.[21]

Women start a micro-financing bank to help other women...

Nearly 80,000 women in Rajnandgaon in Chattisgarh have come together to form self-help groups and start a successful micro-banking initiative. Known as the *Maa Bamleshwari Bank*, it has 5,372 branches and reaches out to every village in this district. Each self-help group is a branch that raises its own resources and makes its own decisions about lending. Within a year the bank, wholly managed and operated by women, has raised Rs 1.19 crore and disbursed Rs 70 lakh in loans in types and sizes that public-sector banks would not even think of.

"We give loans for everything from pregnancy, vaccination and medical care to buying a second-hand cycle," says Swati Agarwal, a member of one of the groups. The loans vary in size from Rs 200 for buying seeds to Rs 10,000 for buying tractor parts. The campaign is controlled by the women of the district and does not depend on government aid.[22]

Education and grit makes all the difference for Anita...

Born in the backwaters of Bihar, and that too in the lower section of the caste pyramid, it was expected that Anita Kushwaha would shepherd goats, stay away from school and marry young. Her father, Janardhan Singh, a poorly-paid employee at a grocery shop, was determined to make Anita follow what girls had always been doing in Bochaha village of Bihar's Muzaffarpur district.

But one person did not agree: Anita. She wanted to break the shackles. Now, at 21 and in the final year of a Bachelor course, Anita is an established honey-trader with an annual turnover of Rs 2.5 lakh. It was hardly easy. Anita won her first battle when, as a six-year-old, a local teacher and she persuaded her parents to let her attend school. "It wasn't just our argument; my parents agreed because education till Class V was free," says Anita. Since they were incapable of meeting their daughter's schooling expenses after Class V, Anita began teaching children to pay for her education. She also took to running errands for honeykeepers from neighbouring villages who would visit her locality thanks to the litchi trees. "That's how I learned bee-keeping," Anita says. Fired by ambition and troubled by her poverty, she took to beekeeping full time. Using her savings of Rs 5,000 from tuitions and some money from her mother, Rekha Devi, she set up her business in 2002, with two bee-boxes and as many queen bees. In just a few months, she had made a significant profit.

Anita was stung by bees many times and her swollen face would be an object of ridicule. But she kept going. "People would ask me if I get stung. Yes, I'd say. 'Does it hurt?' Yes, I'd say," she says. But it does not matter now. Anita's father left his job to join her business and visits other districts with the bee-boxes to collect honey from different sources.

Anita is studying for an English literature degree and she has made her parents promise not to arrange her marriage until she has completed her college degree. A pucca house has replaced their modest dwelling and Anita has gifted a motor-cycle to her younger brother. Her improved social standing is reflected in the fact that her mother is now the village chief of a political party. Her success has inspired other families to take to beekeeping and, remarkably, every girl in her village goes to school now.[23]

These are inspiring stories of courageous people
trying to make a difference.
We can all choose to be instruments of change;
we can all play a part in transforming
the future of our daughters,
in transforming our own future.

7

Empowering Women

Our deepest fear is not that we are inadequate.
Our deepest fear is that we are powerful
Beyond measure.
It is our light, not our darkness that most frightens us.
We ask ourselves, who am I to be
Brilliant, gorgeous, talented and fabulous?
Actually, who are you not to be?
You are a child of God.
Your playing small doesn't serve the world.
There is nothing enlightened about shrinking,
So that other people won't feel insecure around you.
We were born to make manifest
The glory of God that is within us.
It's not just in some of us; it's in everyone.
And as we let our light shine,
We unconsciously give other people permission
To do the same.
  Marriane Williamson

If we have been blessed with a woman in our life, we have been given a precious gift. It is our simple human duty to love her, nurture her and respect her. And given her present low status in much of Indian society, it is our responsibility to help her empower herself.

It is important to understand what an empowered woman is, so we can be enthusiastic about liberating our women, not fearful of this idea. An empowered woman has self-confidence and high self-esteem. She respects herself and invites others to treat her with dignity and respect. She is capable of being self-sufficient, whether she works outside the home or not. She is considerate, compassionate and has a great capacity to love. Empowered women provide tremendous support and strength to men; they do not overpower them. They enrich the world around them with their presence and purpose.

> Study after study has shown us that when women are fully empowered and engaged, all of society benefits.
>
> *Asha-Rose Migiro, United Nations*
> *Deputy Secretary-General*

India has been a patriarchy for a long time, but it is time now to move forward; it is time to develop into a society that is neither male-dominated, nor female-dominated, but where men and women are equal – socially, politically and economically. This is not an impossible dream. There are many Western societies, patriarchal until just a few decades ago, which have made great strides towards achieving this dream. We can do it too.

There are some simple things we can do to break away from prevailing customs to transform the lives of the women around us.

▪ *Let us say no to dowry*

To demand dowry or to accept gifts which are "freely given" by a girl's family are such an accepted norm that most people do not even think they are doing something wrong or potentially hurtful. In fact, dowry has such a powerful social sanction that the boy's family does not hesitate to openly talk about what they are getting (*"das lakh ki party hai"* – a proposal has come from a girl's family willing to give 10 lakhs of rupees) and the wedding guests feel no awkwardness when they "view" the dowry which the girl's family has had to display for all to see. To break a social custom that has become so entrenched will take great courage.

The power to break this social evil rests with the young men of today and their parents. To demand dowry is wrong. To accept gifts, even if they are not asked for, is wrong. Dowry reduces a woman to a commodity – an item to be bartered. When we indulge in it, we weaken her and her family from the very outset, and true love and harmony can never flourish in such an atmosphere. Allowing a woman to be truly equal is the hallmark of a strong, secure man.

> Any young man who makes dowry a condition of marriage discredits his education and his country and dishonours womanhood.
>
> *Mahatma Gandhi*

The girl's parents no doubt experience great societal pressure to give dowry. However, if we have not been asked for a dowry and we are giving it anyway, we are doing our daughter a great disservice. Why must we "sweeten the pot" when we get her married? Are our daughters not a gift in themselves? Why is it only the girl's parents' obligation to give the couple a good start? Should this not come equally from both sides?

To the extent possible, let us try to be more concerned with our daughter's welfare than with what society will say. The duty of a girl's parents is to give her a good education and a strong moral framework. After that, it is up to the young couple to make a life for themselves on the strength of their own hard work and merit. When we lavish the boy's family with expensive gifts, these gifts create an expectation and perpetuate a power imbalance that our daughters will never be able to break.

▪ Let us offer to share the expense of our son's marriage

Why have we blindly accepted the tradition that the girl's family must bear the entire expense of the wedding? Does it seem either right or fair? Could not both the boy's family and girl's family share the expenses so the entire burden does not fall on her parents? If we have a son we can make this choice and start a new tradition.

▪ Let's keep marriages simple

Some families cannot afford expensive weddings and the societal pressure to throw a lavish wedding creates a burden of debt that takes years to repay. Some families have been blessed with an excess of wealth and they rationalize: why should we not spend this money on a much beloved daughter? Perhaps we should ask ourselves: what is the motivation behind throwing a lavish wedding? Is it love for our daughter, or our own ego raising its head, urging us to show off our status, wealth and success? A lavish wedding and expensive gifts are *not* a symbol of our love for our daughter.

If we have an excess of wealth, we can consider quietly giving it to the couple when they need the help or giving it away in charity. The world will not know about it, but the Lord will. For the benefit of all society, marriages are best kept as simple as possible. Simplicity, modesty and understatement are great virtues.

■ *Let us not marry off our daughters before they are of age*

Without a doubt there is tremendous societal pressure to marry off our daughters early. Without a doubt the safety of our unmarried daughters is a concern. But a girl below eighteen years of age is just a child. At that age, she is extremely vulnerable to abuse and mistreatment in her husband's home. Early pregnancy and childbirth ruin her health and are, in fact, a risk to her life. Besides, this child loses the precious opportunity to gain an education and develop her personality. Most importantly, she loses her childhood, the few carefree, joyful years she could have had before the responsibilities of marriage and parenthood commence.

■ *Let's be supportive of a daughter who raises her voice against abuse*

Very often, young women suffer in silence because we, the society around her, do not support her and her parents. Crimes against women and dowry-related abuse go unreported because these young women are afraid we would judge them harshly. Let us try to be less judgmental and more supportive of the daughters in our community.

- ***Let's treat our daughters-in-law as we would
  our own daughters***

Let's welcome our new daughter-in-law into the family with
joy and give her the same love and respect we give our own son.
This will help create an atmosphere of peace, love and harmony
in our home.

- ***Let's not blame our wife or daughter-in-law
  if she is unable to conceive a son***

If a woman is unable to conceive, her husband could be equally
responsible. If a woman is unable to conceive a *son*, she is not
at all responsible. *A woman has absolutely nothing to do with the
gender of the child; her husband is entirely responsible.*

- ***Let us not sex-select***

Do not conduct a sex-detection test. Do not keep having
daughters or multiple abortions of daughters in your attempt to
beget a son. Have at most two children as our country advises,
and if the Lord wills that they shall be daughters, so be it.

- ***Let's give our daughters the same education
  and opportunities we give our sons***

Girls are as intelligent as boys and as capable as them. The
results of school examinations and the administrative services
exams regularly show the outstanding performance of girls with
many of them topping the merit list. The benefits of educating
our daughters are far-reaching. There is a well-said dictum:
Educate a man and you educate one person; educate a woman
and you educate a whole family. Studies show that girls who
receive just one year of education more than the current average
boost their eventual wages by between 10% and 20%.[24]

So give your daughter the same quality of education you give your son. Give her the same opportunities to learn new things. Give her the tools to stand on her own feet and earn independently. We have been given the gift of reason and choice. Through education, let us give our daughters the same gift: the ability to reason and the power to choose.

■ *Let's encourage our daughter or wife*
  to work outside the home

Self-sufficiency gives a woman confidence, liberty, identity, security, status and a feeling of sharing in the economic needs of a household.

Working outside the home and earning an independent income tend to have a clear impact on enhancing the social standing of a woman in the household and the society. Her contribution to the prosperity of the family is then more visible, and she also has more voice, because of being less dependent

on others. Further, outside employment often has useful edu-
cational effects, in terms of exposure to the world outside the
household.

Dr Amartya Sen
Development as Freedom

There are many women, however, who choose not to work
outside the home because financially they can afford not to, and
personally they feel fulfilled in their role as home-makers. Let
us give equal value to a woman's role as a professional and as a
homemaker, irrespective of the choice she makes.

■ *Let us support a woman when she loses her husband*

How can we hold a woman responsible for bringing bad luck into
the family and causing her husband's death? Aren't the breaths
he is destined to breathe determined even before he is born?

Let us do our utmost to support her and her children during
this difficult time, both financially and emotionally. And let us
encourage these women to remarry, so they may start life anew.

■ *Let us appreciate our wife and mother*

Women, especially those who do not work outside the home,
almost unanimously feel they have thankless jobs. There are a
myriad small details that go into their jobs – from tying shoelaces,
to buying new clothes for ever-growing children, to making cups
of tea, to making a phone call to a sick relative – none of which
seem to amount to anything. We know now, that over time all
these little things amount to a lot: they create well-brought-up
children, happy homes, and strong family relationships; these
actions are, in fact, the glue that creates strong, bonded families

and communities. However, while a woman is performing these actions, she feels unappreciated and taken for granted.

Do what you can to make your wife or mother feel appreciated, help her with some of her chores, and watch your relationship become transformed. Simple acts of appreciation will radiate well-being into the home.

■ Let's give our daughters an equal share in the inheritance

Why do we feel our daughters cannot inherit the family property or the family business? Are our daughters not part of the family? What is the harm if our daughter inherits our wealth?

When you convey a clear message to all your children that your daughter will inherit an equal share, you empower her immeasurably.

When you cut a daughter out of an equal share in the inheritance you send a signal of unequal love and value.

■ Let us raise enlightened sons

The biggest hope for change lies with future generations. Let's treat sons and daughters in the same home with equal love and fairness, teach brothers to respect and honour their sisters, and raise our sons to believe that women are equal to men in all respects. This is a fundamental shift that has the potential to save the next generation of women. This crucial responsibility has been entrusted to the parents of sons.

■ Let us give our daughters the ultimate gift: high self-esteem

Today, our daughters are part of a society that idolizes sons. Right from childhood, girls are made to accept the norms of a patriarchal and male-dominated society and they grow up accepting themselves to be inferior to boys. The greatest gift you can give your daughter is to empower her with high self-esteem. The way to do this is to treat her as an equal: love her equally, educate her equally, and give her equal opportunities. Encourage her to achieve more, to assume responsibilities that are normally considered to be in the male domain. And let's make it clear from the very beginning that she will get an equal share in the inheritance.

A young woman with high self-esteem will go on to make you proud. She will have the courage to say no to pressure over dowry; she will have the courage to say no if there is pressure to have a sex-detection test; she will have the courage to say no if she is asked to abort her baby daughter. She will be independent and self-sufficient. She will expect to be treated with respect and she will raise a daughter who has high self-esteem as well.

A young woman empowered with high self-esteem will be a catalyst of change.

> I was my parent's *laadli* (beloved daughter). It is because of my parents' upbringing that I am what I am today. It entirely depends upon the parents, on how they bring up

their girl-child. Educate her, make her financially self-reliant and give her the self-respect she deserves...If you [parents] think that your girls are weak, it is not them but your upbringing which is weak. If my parents had the same thought process, I wouldn't be who I am today. Their thinking was strong and therefore I grew up to be a strong individual. You can also do the same. Bring up your girl-child with care. Make her self-reliant. Self-reliance will come with education and self-reliance is power. If you do this your girl-children will respect you more and will care for you for life.

Kiran Bedi, India's first female police officer [25]

A woman with high self-esteem has the power to fundamentally change our society because today's daughter is tomorrow's mother and mother-in-law. If girls are taught to value themselves and boys are taught to value girls and women as equals, we will finally be able to rid ourselves as a society of the evils of inequality and oppression.

■ Let's uphold the laws of the land

The law of the land could not be more clear: It is illegal to sex-select. Under this broad missive, there are several others: it is illegal to conduct a sex-detection test; it is illegal to advertise sex-detection tests; it is illegal to run an unregistered clinic. By the same token, it is equally illegal to give or take dowry.

Let us uphold the laws of our land.

■ Let's raise awareness about sex-selection

Although many people are aware that sex-selection occurs in our country, very few are aware of the scale at which it is being practised and of the horrific social consequences of allowing it to continue unchecked.

So spread the word among neighbours, friends and relatives, and spread the word among "influencers" – teachers, doctors, lawyers, judges, politicians, administrators and the media. Awareness of the crisis is the first step. Inequality and sex-selection will only stop when the call against them becomes a national crusade.

Society must do its part to treat women fairly, equally and compassionately. But in the end, women themselves must understand one fundamental fact: the most basic and important things in life, like freedom, equality and empowerment cannot be given by others; they have to be taken. Like spirituality, they have to be worked for, understood, and struggled for. It is only after striving for our freedom and empowerment that we will realize how important it is to us, and we will work to protect it and hold on to it. If it is just handed to us on a platter, we will not understand its value and it will be easily lost.

———————■———————

Society will help us,
but it is up to us women
to organise our strengths,
individually and collectively;
it is up to us to reach out
and empower ourselves.

———————■———————

8

An Awakening

The journey of a thousand miles
begins with a single step.

Tao Te Ching

The dictionary defines an "awakening" as a recognition, realisation, or coming into an awareness of something. Our current situation calls upon us, whoever we are, to awaken to our highest human potential. If we awaken and live life with spiritual values, we will experience that we are all members of one human family irrespective of gender, race or creed. The dangerous consequences of our present perceptions and priorities demand that we awaken as a matter of extreme urgency.

Throughout history, exceptional people have reminded us of humanity's essentially noble and loving nature. Whether Buddha, Lord Mahavir, the prophets of Judaism, or Jesus; whether Guru Nanak and the Gurus of his line, or the Sufis and the prophets of Islam; whether Mahatma Gandhi, Mother Teresa, Nelson Mandela, or other beacons of the highest human behaviour – indeed any of the myriad exemplars of a spiritualized humanity – such people have illumined the human being's essential loving nature. Their lives inspire us to liberate ourselves, like them, from self-interest and cruelty. They invite us by their example to awaken to our noble potential and build, step by step, a spiritualized, positive world. Our daughters need us to awaken. They need us to react to this present outrage of confusion and wrong thinking. They need us to rethink our social norms and traditions. They need our courage, commitment, and clarity, and most importantly our love; they need us to treat them as equals to their brothers.

Let us pledge to be catalysts of change. Let us pledge to live as awakened and enlightened human beings and nurture, cherish and empower the women in our lives. And let us do this not just for women but for our own sake as well. As we instinctively know, all living beings are intricately interconnected. There can be no act of cruelty that does not ultimately reflect back to us. And likewise, the effect of every act of kindness and compassion ripples back to us.

If we could find it in our hearts to treat our daughters as equal to our sons, the universe would shower its blessings on us. And our daughters would return that love many times over. This attitude of love and acceptance has the power to transform both us and our society.

Our small book invites us – all of us – to awaken and respond to the world around us in a way that is aligned with our own essential divinity.

Wake Up, My Friend

Wake up, my friend,
Life revolves on the wheel of do and be done by –
Give and take, act and react –
Yet there's a different way of being,
A way to break free from the cycle

A way to break free from the cycle
Your human life offers an opportunity,
To awaken and expand your perspective,
Be aware of life's sacred heart

Be aware of life's sacred heart,
Be mindful of what you do,
Choose your deeds with utmost caution,
Align your actions with life's heart, with love

Align your actions with life's heart, with love,
This moment is a chance in eternity –
By what you do shift from ignorance to understanding,
Walk the way of liberation

Walk the way of liberation,
Be true and compassionate to all,
You yourself will become godlike,
You yourself – be divine.

M. F. Singh

A Final Note
Murder on a Mass Scale

*At the beginning of every action, look
at its end, so that you should not have
to repent on the day of judgment.*
Maulana Rum

The human mindset is deeply rooted; to avoid having to take action, we easily gloss over what we do not want to know. To emphasize the acute urgency of the need for change, this chapter presents you with the devastating statistics that have resulted from our low value for women. If we valued women as equal to men, these statistics and the reality on the ground would not be what they are.

1. The Scale of the Crisis

Killing a living being is killing oneself; compassion towards creatures is compassion towards oneself.

Lord Mahavira

They say a picture can convey more than a thousand words. The following graphs paint a very real picture of what has been happening to our daughters in the decade of the nineties, and allows us to project in our own minds how much worse the figures will be in the Census of 2011 if we do not reverse this appalling trend immediately.

1. *The child sex ratio has been steadily declining over the past 40 years.*

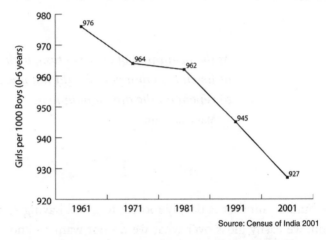

Source: Census of India 2001

This trend will continue to haunt the society for decades to come unless course corrective steps are taken.

Registrar General of India, Census

2. *Sex-selection is more prevalent in urban areas than in rural areas.*

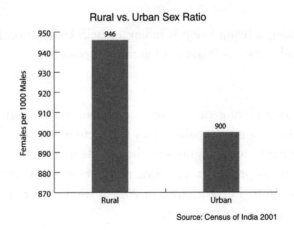

Source: Census of India 2001

3. *Educated families are aborting babies at a faster pace than illiterate families.*

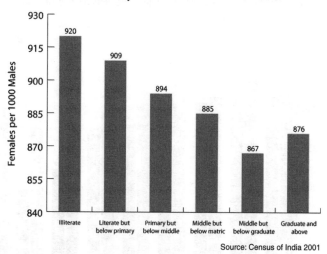

Sex Ratio at Birth by Level of Education of the Mother

Source: Census of India 2001

4. *Sex-selection occurs across all religions.*

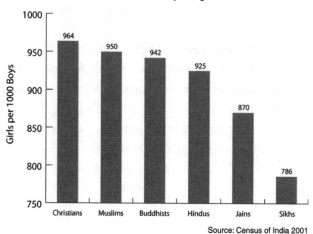

Child Sex Ratio by Religion

Source: Census of India 2001

5. *National averages hide steep declines and critically low ratios in certain regions.*

States/Union Territories with the highest decline in Child Sex Ratio

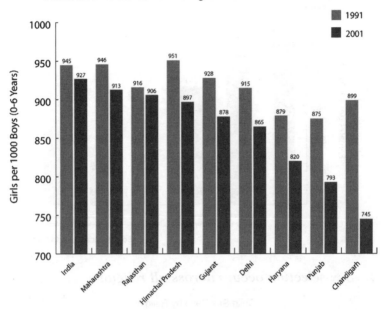

Source: Census of India 2001

Just as throughout history euphemisms have been used to mask mass killings, terms like "female foeticide," "son-preference" and "sex-selection" are now being used to cover up what amount to illegal contract killings on a massive scale, with the contracts being between parents and doctors somehow justified as a form of consumer choice.

Dr Puneet Bedi, obstetrician, activist,
as quoted by Christine Toomey,
"Gender Genocide" *The Sunday Times*, August 2007

6. *Globally our sex ratio is among the lowest and predicted to soon be lower than China's.*

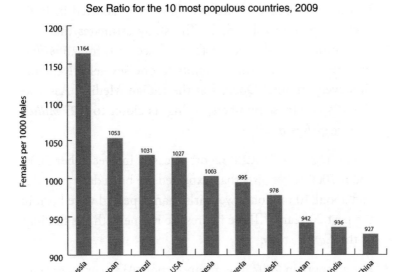

Sex Ratio for the 10 most populous countries, 2009

Source: Population Division of the Department of Economic and Social Affairs
of the United Nations Secretariat, World Population Prospects: The 2008 Revision

As long as this indifference continues our numbers of missing girls will continue to increase. And in the next 10 years we are very likely to exceed China in terms of having the country with the largest number of girls eliminated before birth.

Dr Sabu George, activist, as quoted by
Steve Herman, *Voice of America*, March 05, 2007

More current indicators of scale

- In 2006, the prestigious British Medical Journal, *The Lancet*, published a study that argued that as many as 10 million unborn female babies may have been aborted in India over the past two decades.[26] The study estimates that sex-determination and selective abortion accounts for *0.5 million missing girls yearly*. This amounts to one sex-selective abortion every minute! Doctors at the Indian Medical Association dispute these numbers, saying its closer to *0.25 million missing girls yearly.*[27]

- According to a UNICEF report released in December 2006, about 7000 fewer girls than expected are born daily in India, and about 10 million fewer girls than expected were born in the past 20 years.[28] These figures are in line with the findings of the *Lancet* study.

- For a report in 2007, the group Action Aid sent interviewers to 6000 households in five regions of north India. In one state, researchers found rural areas with just 500 girls for every 1000 boys, and communities of high-caste, urban families with just 300 girls per 1000 boys.[29]

- *The Pioneer,* October 28, 2001, reported that the 200-odd Rathore families in Western Rajasthan's Barmer district have 2 to 4 male children each on average. There are only 2 girls in the entire clan. At a conservative estimate, the ratio is 400 male children to 2 female children.[30]

We will have a better idea about the exact scale of the crisis only after the next census in 2011. In the meanwhile, while the experts argue over the numbers, girls are being eliminated every day.

2. IMPLEMENTING THE LAW OF THE LAND

The rights of others you do not understand;
Burdened with a load of ill-gotten wealth,
  you will have to return to the creation.
Robbed of a priceless opportunity,
  in the gambling den of the world,
  you are going to lose a winning hand.

Saa'in Bulleh Shah

Recognizing the need for safe abortion services, the government enacted the Medical Termination of Pregnancies Act (MTP Act) in 1971. It is an important aspect of protecting women from unwanted or dangerous pregnancies which they often face. However, although abortion is legal under the MTP Act, sex-selection (conducting a sex-detection test and aborting the foetus if it is a girl) is absolutely illegal under the newer Pre-Conception & Pre-Natal Diagnostics Techniques (PC & PNDT) Act which was enacted in 1994 and amended in 2003. Most experts agree that this Act, despite its problems, is actually a comprehensive and effective piece of legislation. The problem lies with its implementation.

Illegal to sex-select

According to the Act, it is illegal to conduct a sex-detection test.

If half a million girls are aborted every year, it can be assumed that at least one million illegal sex-detection tests are performed each year since only one out of every two tests on average will reveal that the baby is a girl.

Clinics must be registered

Any Genetic Clinic, Counseling Centre, or Laboratory, conducting these tests must be registered under the Act.

> Today there are over 30,000 registered ultrasound clinics in India.[31] It is estimated there could be 2 to 3 times as many in operation illegally. There are thousands of ultrasound machines installed in vans and on motorcycles by profiteers who travel from village to village charging rural families exorbitant fees for the procedure.

Illegal to indicate the sex of the child

The law states that no person conducting the test should communicate to the pregnant woman or her relatives the sex of the foetus using words or signs, or in any other manner.

> Doctors continue to communicate the sex of the foetus, clearly banned by the Act, through an innovative coded language:
> "It's time to buy blue clothes," "Go buy pedas," or "Jai Shri Krishna," if the foetus is a boy.
> "It's time to buy pink clothes," "Go buy burfis," or "Jai mata di," if the foetus is a girl.
>
> *PC & PNDT Act, A Handbook for the Public*[30]

Illegal to advertise

Any form of advertisement of sex-determination tests is illegal.

Some doctors' billboards continue to advertise with statements like "Invest Rs 5000 now and save Rs 5 lakh later," to encourage parents to abort female foetuses and save on a future dowry.

Punishment

Contravening the provisions of the Act can lead to a penalty, which in May 2008, was increased to anywhere between Rs 3–7 lakh. Additionally perpetrators can face jail terms of 3 months to 3 years.

The law was enacted in 1994, yet the very first conviction of a doctor, sentenced to two years in prison for violating the Act, was in March, 2006.[32]

Are women getting justice?

Missing women
Over 50 million

Cases filed under the Act till Dec 2007[33]
Total cases filed: 416
Convictions: 15

*Can a law that is out of step with the social will
ever be effectively implemented?*

The Law of the Land is Up Against Big Business

- In India today, sex-detection and selection is an over Rs 400 crore business and growing.[27]

- Medical professionals have benefitted from promoting the technology for decades. It is no coincidence that no medical association has taken a strong stand to curb the unethical use of diagnostic procedures. In fact the medical lobby is powerful and has fought to control their commercial interests. Doctors have even gone to court against the law.

- While some ultrasound manufacturers take care to ensure they only sell to registered clinics, a vast number of machines are sold without the necessary paperwork.

- Ultrasound machines are used not just for sex-detection, but also for very important medical purposes: detecting abnormalities in the foetus, protecting mother and child from harm, and for several non-gynaecological purposes like detecting cancers, etc. However the demand for ultrasound machines has exploded over the past 20 years due to the enormous demand for sex-detection tests, and multinational companies have been flooding the market with machines to meet the demand.

- The sale of ultrasound machines in India brought in Rs 308 crore in 2006, a 10% increase over the previous year.[34]

India's Constitution

India is the world's largest democracy. We were one of the first countries to grant women the right to vote (in 1928). Our

Constitution is one of the finest in the world. It promises justice to all; it promises liberty of thought, expression, belief, faith and worship to all. It prohibits discrimination on the grounds of religion, race, caste, sex or place of birth.

Are our women getting their constitutional rights?

* Freedom to lead a long life
* Right to health
* Right to education
* Freedom to work without exploitation
* Freedom to participate in decision-making
* Freedom from fear

When a woman's right to life itself
is taken away,
all these other rights
accorded to her by the Constitution
are effectively meaningless.

3. THE REALITY ON THE GROUND - A CRY FOR HELP

> We think sometimes that poverty is only being hungry,
> naked and homeless. The poverty of being unwanted,
> unloved and uncared for is the greatest poverty. We must
> start in our own homes to remedy this kind of poverty.
>
> *Mother Teresa*

The numbers, graphs and statistics can never truly tell the real story – the story of the pain a woman suffers. The purpose of the following excerpts is not to judge anyone; the purpose is to urge us to really see what is going on in the lives of our daughters; the purpose is to move us, so we feel compelled to help.

Dreams of a happily married life...

For nineteen-year-old Reena dreams of a happily married life were never to be. Barely a month after her marriage, she was allegedly tortured and then set ablaze by her in-laws for dowry in Indiranagar in the small hours of Saturday. Daughter of the late Ghanshyam Chand, a fish contractor who expired a year ago, Reena was married to Sunil on April 19th...However, soon after the marriage, Sunil's father demanded a colour television instead of a black and white one and a motorcycle as well. When Reena's mother failed to meet their demands, the teenage housewife was subjected to severe physical torture, allegedly by her husband and mother-in-law...On Saturday morning Reena's mother was informed that Reena was charred to death when a kerosene lamp accidentally fell on her and her clothes caught fire. However, prima-facie it appeared that the victim

was first attacked as her teeth were found broken. Injuries were
also apparent on her wrist and chest.

Times of India, Lucknow,
May 27, 2001 [Names changed]

Aulad te munda hi hoonda hai...

Veero (not her real name) looks anaemic and malnourished and
years older than her 34 years. If one half of her life has been
spent yearning for a son and having four abortions, one after the
other, the rest of it is full of regret for not having anybody who
will give her *"paani te aag"* (to perform the last rites). *"Munde de
bina maa-peo rul jande ne"* (Without a son, parents are ruined),
she says, her eyes brimming over with tears and unknown fears
lurking in them. Her three daughters are not hers: *"Aulad te
munda hi hoonda hai. Kudiyan te beganiyan hoondian."* (Only a
son is truly one's child. Daughters belong to others.)

Aruti Nayar, "Silent Genocide"
The Tribune, May 6, 2001

In a shocking discovery...

In a shocking discovery, the Orissa police on July 23, 2007,
recovered as many as 30 polythene bags stuffed with female foetuses and the body parts of newborn babies from a dry well near
a private clinic in Nayagarh, close to Bhubaneswar...A report
said that the police searched the well after seven female foetuses
packed into polythene bags were found dumped in a deserted
area in a nearby village in mid-July 2007. The police haven't
ruled out a link between the two incidents and are suspecting a

female foeticide racket…This discovery is just part of an unending series of female foeticides that have been happening in several parts of the country. In June 2007, a doctor was arrested on charges of illegally aborting 260 female foetuses after police recovered bones from the septic tank in the basement of his maternity clinic in the outskirts of New Delhi.

"No End for Female Foeticides in India"
Dance with Shadows, 24 July, 2007

No mother wants her child to die, but…

At a workshop in a remote village in Rajasthan, a woman who had come with her 8-month-old son and 3-year-old daughter suddenly found the son ill with high fever. The boy was struggling to breathe. It was a remote village where there were no medical facilities, and she pointed to her daughter and said, "I wish this had happened to her."

Anyway, the boy was shifted to a hospital the next day and got well. Later, when I told her I was disturbed by her comment, she said, "Look, if my daughter had died, I would have still been allowed to go back home. But if my son, born after four daughters, had died, there was no way I could return home. I would have had to commit suicide, there is no way the family would have accepted me, because this is a prized son."

No mother likes to kill her child, but this is the way women live; their pain is determined by other forces; they cannot decide when to mourn, whose death to mourn and how to mourn. These are the realities on the ground.

Abha Bhaiya of *Jagori*, as quoted by
Rasheeda Bhagat, "Slaughter in the Womb"

Safai kara di...

A woman upon being told that her child is healthy and beautiful looks away sullenly. A nurse explains, "It's a girl, that's why." In another part of the country, a woman sits worriedly in the gynaecology ward of a hospital. She is seven months pregnant. An ultrasound scan has told her it's a boy and she doesn't want to lose "her baby." About her earlier two pregnancies she says, *"Donon time test mein ladki nikli to safai kara di."* (Both times the test revealed it was a girl so I had them "cleaned out.")

Justice Y. K. Sabharwal, Chief Justice of India,
in his speech, "Eradication of Female Foeticide"

Girls are sold...

Trafficking of women from Assam to Punjab and Haryana has been on the rise due to the skewed sex-ratio in these two states. In some cases minor girls in batches of four or five who have been trafficked from Assam are openly put up for sale at prices ranging from Rs 10,000 to Rs 30,000 in some panchayats of Haryana. Such girls are known as *Paros* in Haryana.

Ravi Kant, Executive Director of *Shakti Vahini*,
as quoted by Sushanta Talukdar,
"Trafficking of Women from Assam on the Rise"

Unanswered prayers...

Thirty-six year old Sukhraj Singh works as a labourer in a dairy farm in Milan, Italy, but he is in Amritsar on a mission. Childless for the last seven years, he and his wife came down to the Bir Baba Budha Mandir to pray for a son. However, last year when his wife had a baby daughter both husband and wife were shattered. So this year they're back again – to ask for the son they never had.

"We prayed at this temple and then we had a daughter. So we have come back again to this temple, this time I want a male child," he says…For years people from India and abroad have been flocking to temples and gurudwaras like this one, spread all across Punjab in the hope of a male child. Visitors here say that asking for a girl is not even an option…

This is evident when one sees 19-year-old Rajwant Kaur visiting these temples to pray for a brother – she seems to know she is a burden on her family. "No one wants a girl anymore. Everyone wants just boys and that's because often parents can't pay the dowry so they pray that no girls are born into the family," she says.

Nilanjana Bose, CNN IBN, "Son Temples of Punjab"

I wish I had a daughter…

"It is the will of God that only sons are born in this household now," says Balvir Kaur as her husband hovers in the background. "We don't feel disturbed by this. The main reason is to keep property in the family. We have to learn how to cope. Earlier there was infanticide, now there is foeticide," she says, adding quickly that this had not happened in her family. Only when Balvir moves away and leaves me briefly with her daughter-in-law Kulwinder, does a hint of sadness enter the conversation. "I wish I had a daughter," she says. "A woman feels awful without a daughter. Daughters help their mothers. I still feel sad about it," she says, looking away. "But there were miscarriages."

Christine Toomey, "Gender Genocide"
The Sunday Times, August 26, 2007
At the village of Dera Mir Miran
Sex Ratio 361 (Census 2001)

GIFT OF LIFE

When a son is born, drums of joy we beat,
When a daughter is born, we mourn in grief!

Let's give our sweet daughter the gift of life...

Why do we murder her in the womb?
Why do we stifle her innocent screams?
What is her fault, after all?
Differences between boy and girl,
We have created them all.

When a son is born, drums of joy we beat,
When a daughter is born, we mourn in grief!

Why do we inflict such pain on our girls?
Why do we reject this gift from the Lord?
Why have we snuffed out the light in two homes?
Without shame we trade her away for a price.
In the large dowry market we make profit from boys,
No fear of the Lord, no fear of Law,
In our greed for wealth, we forget it all.

Let's give our sweet daughter the gift of life...

The source of all life, the power of love,
The coolness of shade, the soul of the family,
The safety of mother's lap...who can forget?
Her eyes brimming with love, who can forget?
The cuddles of a daughter, the love of a wife,
The blessings of a mother...Who can forget?

Let's give our sweet daughter the gift of life...

Give her the wealth of a great education.
Give her equal opportunities, a great foundation.
Give her the respect and esteem you give all.
Is a daughter less than anyone, after all?

She's been head of the village, president, prime minister,
Astronaut, doctor, professor, engineer, she has been,
In science, in spirituality, in literature and the arts,
In every sphere she's succeeded, she's won.

Why do we murder her in the womb?
Why do we stifle this innocent's screams?

Change! Old attitudes – it is time to change them.
Change! Old customs – it is time to change them.
Awaken! And listen to the voice of your conscience.
Be fearless! Have faith in the all-knowing Lord.
Become a good human in the eyes of the Lord.

When the Lord is one and our soul is of the Lord,
Then why this distinction between women and men?

Let's give our sweet daughter the gift of life...

Then one day, drums will reverberate,
Daughters and sons, both, we will celebrate!

Let's give our sweet daughter the gift of life...

Mom, Dad,
It is you who brought me into this world.
Give me a chance.

Souls are not male or female.
You are as beautiful and as powerful
as any other soul in the universe.

Dr Brian L. Weiss

SOURCES AND REFERENCES

1. Research study in 2005 by Caliper, a USA-based consulting firm, and Aurora, a UK-based firm, "How Women are Redefining Leadership;" Pew Research Center, 2008, "Men or Women: Who's the Better Leader?"
2. 2001 Census of India.
3. UNICEF Report: "State of the World's Children – 2009."
4. UNICEF India, Newsline: Roopa Bakshi, April 2006, "UNICEF Unveils New Tool to Combat Maternal Mortality in India."
5. UNFPA Report: "State of World Population 2004, Adolescents and Young People: Key Health and Development Concerns."
6. National Family Health Survey (2005–2006) Report.
7. Kalyani Menon-Sen and A. K. Shiva Kumar, 2001, "Women in India: How Free? How Equal?" A Report commissioned by the United Nations Resident Coordinator in India.
8. National Centre for Labour, 1999.
9. Srilata Swaminathan, "Female Foeticide: Facts and Figures."
10. INCLEN Survey 2000, "Indian Studies of Abuse in the Family Environment, 1998–2000," A study conducted by IndiaSAFE and the Indian branch of the International Clinical Epidemiology Network (INCLEN).
11. National Centre for Labour, 1999.
12. Aruti Nayar, *The Tribune*, May 6, 2001, "Silent Genocide."
13. National Crime Records Bureau, 2007 statistics.
14. "45 Million Daughters Missing: A Compendium on Research and Intervention on Female Foeticide and Infanticide in India." Published by IFES and EKATRA, funded by USAID (The United States Agency for International Development).
15. UNFPA Report, 1997, "India: Towards Population and Development Goals."
16. UNICEF India, Child Sex Ratio (www.unicef.org/india/CHILD-SEX-RATIOin.pdf).

17. Valerie M. Hudson, Andrea M. den Boer, "Bare Branches: The Security Implications of Asia's Surplus Male Population."
18. Sakshi, 1998, "Justice on Gender."
19. Rita Patel, Department of Maternal and Child Health, School of Public Health, "The Practice of Sex Selective Abortion in India: May You Be the Mother of a Hundred Sons."
20. Dr Meeta Singh, "Outcomes of the Dignity of the Girl Child Program" (Rajasthan University Women's Association & IFES Initiative).
21. Rajesh Sinha, *Indian Express*, May 10, 1998, "After 115 Years A Villages Celebrates the Wedding of a Girl it Did Not Kill."
22. *India Today*, July 15, 2002, "Rural Women Start Successful Micro-Banking Scheme in Chattisgarh."
23. *India Today*, May 1, 2009, Amitabh Srivastava, "Grit and Honey."
24. Centre for Global Development, 2008, "Girls Count: A Global Investment and Action Agenda."
25. *Times of India*, April 10, 2009, Kiran Bedi was interviewed at the Launch of *Laadli Week*, a joint venture between Star Plus and Mahindra's Nanhi Kali Project for educating the girl-child.
26. *The Lancet*, January 2006, "Low Male-to-Female Sex Ratio of Children Born in India: National Survey of 1.1 Million Households."
27. Scott Baldauf, *Christian Science Monitor*, January 13, 2006, "India's 'Girl Deficit' Deepest Among Educated."
28. UNICEF Report: "State of the World's Children, 2007, Women and Children: The Double Dividend of Gender Equality."
29. Tim Sullivan, *News Plus*, April 17, 2008, "India Surges, But Shackles Of Sex-Selection Remain."
30. The Pre-Conception and Pre-Natal Diagnostic Techniques Act 1994, "Answers to Frequently Asked Questions, A Handbook For The Public."
31. *BioEdge (BioEthics News from Around the World)* May 2, 2007, "GE's Ultrasound Machines and India's Gendercide."
32. UNFPA Report: "Missing: Mapping the Adverse Child Sex Ratio in India."
33. *Times of India*, May 4, 2008, Kounteya Sinha, "Government Plans to Crack Down on Sex Determination Tests."
34. *Wall Street Journal*, Peter Wonacott, April 19, 2007, "India's Skewed Sex Ratio Puts GE Sales in Spotlight."

BOOKS AND AUTHORS CITED

Bahu (1629?–1691)   Hazrat Sultan Bahu, a disciple of Sayyid Abdur Rahman Qadiri, was one of the great Sufi saints of the Indian sub-continent. He was not formally educated, but is said to have written more than a hundred works in Persian and Arabic. However, it is his poems in the Punjabi language that live on and remain popular among the people of Punjab.

Bedi, Kiran (1949–)   Kiran Bedi is an Indian social activist and retired Indian police officer. She became the first woman to join the Indian Police Service in 1972. She served in a number of difficult assignments including: Traffic Commissioner of New Delhi, Deputy Inspector General of Police in insurgency prone Mizoram, Director General of the Narcotics Control Bureau and Inspector General of Prisons, Tihar Jail – one of the world's largest prison complexes. Bedi's prison reform policies lead to her winning the prestigious *Ramon Magsaysay Award*. She was last posted as Director General, Bureau of Police Research and Development, where she took voluntary retirement. She has subsequently founded two NGOs in India: *Navjyoti,* for welfare and preventive policing, and *India Vision Foundation* for prison reforms, drug abuse prevention and child welfare.

Bible   The term Bible, or *Holy Bible,* refers to the sacred scriptures of Judaism and Christianity. The Jewish Bible, written in Hebrew, is divided into the Torah (Five Books of Moses), Prophets, and Writings. It recounts the history of mankind from the time of the creation, the lives of the patriarchs and early Israelites, and the teachings of their prophets and holy men. The Christian Bible is made up of the Old Testament, which includes the books of the Jewish Bible, and the New Testament, which consists of writings pertaining to the life and teachings of Jesus Christ and his disciples. It contains the four Gospels (Matthew, Mark, Luke and John), the Epistles (letters from some of the disciples), the Acts of the Apostles, and Revelations (also known as the Apocalypse).

Bonaparte, Napoleon (1769–1821)   Later known as Emperor Napoleon I, Bonaparte was a military and political leader of France whose actions shaped European politics in the early 19th century. Born in Corsica and trained as an artillery officer in mainland France, Bonaparte rose in power until he became Emperor. He turned the armies of the French against every major European power and dominated continental Europe through a series of military victories. He was finally defeated by the Coalition forces in the battle of Waterloo in 1815. He is remembered for the Napoleonic code, which laid the administrative and judicial foundations for much of Western Europe.

Brittain, Vera Mary (1893–1970)   Brittain was an English writer, feminist and pacifist, best remembered as the author of the bestselling 1933 memoir *Testament of Youth*, recounting her experiences during World War I and the growth of her ideology of Christian pacifism.

Bulleh Shah (1680–1758)   Born into a high-class Muslim family, Saa'in Bulleh Shah grew up in Kasur, near Lahore. He incurred the wrath of his community when he became the disciple of the mystic saint Inayat Shah of Lahore, a simple gardener. His poetry and songs of mystical love and longing are still recited and sung in India and Pakistan.

Carlyle, Thomas (1795–1881)   Carlyle was a Scottish satirical writer, essayist, historian and teacher during the Victorian era. He wrote articles for the *Edinburgh Encyclopaedia*, and became a controversial social commentator. Carlyle's books and articles inspired social reformers such as John Ruskin, Charles Dickens, John Burns, Tom Mann and William Morris.

Charan Singh (1916–1990)   Born in Moga, Punjab, Maharaj Charan Singh was a disciple of Maharaj Sawan Singh of Radha Soami Satsang Beas. Hazur Maharaj Ji was a lawyer by profession. In 1951 Maharaj Jagat Singh made him his successor, and for the next four decades Maharaj Ji travelled throughout India and the world, giving discourses and initiating seekers. Teaching the universal path of spirituality, he stressed the need to look beyond differences of race, culture and religion. His teachings have been recorded in several books containing his writings, talks and letters. Before his passing on in 1990, he appointed Gurinder Singh Dhillon as his successor.

Covey, Stephen R. (1932–)   Born in Salt Lake City, Utah, Dr Covey wrote the best-selling book, *The Seven Habits of Highly Effective People*. Other books he has written include *First Things First, Principle-Centered Leadership, The Seven Habits of Highly Effective Families, The 8ᵗʰ Habit* and *The Leader In Me – How Schools and Parents Around the World Are Inspiring Greatness, One Child at a Time*.

Dhammapada *(Path of Truth)*   The author of the verses in the Dhammapada is unknown, although they are believed to be the teachings of the Buddha himself. The text of the book was established by the time of the great Buddhist Emperor, Ashoka, in the third century BC.

Einstein, Albert (1879–1955)   An American physicist born in Germany, Einstein was awarded the *Nobel Prize for Physics* in 1921. Although he is best known for his theory of relativity, he published more than 300 scientific works and more than 150 non-scientific works. Einstein believed that spiritual experience is the driving force behind scientific research. In 1999, *Time* magazine named him "Person of the Century." In the words of Einstein biographer Don Howard, "to the scientifically literate and the public at large Einstein is synonymous with genius."

Frankl, Viktor Emil (1905–1997)   An Austrian neurologist and psychiatrist as well as a Holocaust survivor, Frankl founded logotherapy, which is a form of Existential Analysis, the "Third Viennese School of Psychotherapy." His best-selling book, *Man's Search for Meaning,* chronicles his experiences as a concentration camp inmate and describes his psychotherapeutic method of finding meaning in all forms of existence, even the most sordid ones, and thus a reason to continue living. Frankl, who had personal contact with Sigmund Freud and Alfred Adler, was one of the key figures in existential therapy.

Gandhi, Mohandas Karamchand (1869–1948)   Gandhi was a prominent political and spiritual leader of India and the Indian independence movement. He was the pioneer of *satyagraha* – upholding truth by resisting tyranny through mass civil disobedience, firmly founded upon ahimsa or total non-violence – which led India to independence and inspired movements for civil rights and freedom across the world. He is commonly known around the world as Mahatma Gandhi. He is officially honoured in India as the Father of the Nation. His birthday, 2nd October, is commemorated in India as a national holiday, and worldwide as the International Day of Non-Violence.

Goethe, Johann Wolfgang von (1749–1832)   Goethe was a German writer and according to George Eliot, "Germany's greatest man of letters." Goethe's work spans the fields of poetry, drama, literature, theology, philosophy, humanism and science. His magnum opus, lauded as one of the peaks of world literature, is the two-part drama, *Faust.* Goethe's influence spread across Europe, and his works were a major source of inspiration in music, drama, poetry and philosophy. He is considered to be the most important writer in the German language and one of the most important thinkers in Western culture.

Gourmont, Rémy de (1858–1915)   De Gourmont was a French Symbolist poet and novelist who was widely read in his era. He was also a literary critic of great importance and admired by T. S. Eliot and Ezra Pound in that capacity. De Gourmont came from a publishing family from Cotentin. He was the son of Count Auguste-Marie de Gourmont and his countess, Mathilde de Montfort. He studied law at Caen after which he moved to Paris and was employed at the Bibliothèque Nationale.

Guru Arjun Dev (1563–1606)   Guru Arjun Dev was the fifth Guru in the line of Guru Nanak. Through great effort, Guru Arjun Dev collected, classified and compiled the writings of the *Adi Granth*, including compositions of saints from all over the Indian sub-continent whose teachings emphasize the oneness of God, the path of the Word, the equality of all people, and the pursuit of truth.

Guru Nanak (1469–1539)   Born at Talwandi near Lahore in present-day Pakistan, Guru Nanak Dev spent a large part of his life travelling to spread the teachings of the Word or Divine Name. He was the first in the line of the ten Gurus whose teachings are recorded in the *Adi Granth*, which has become the sacred scripture of the Sikhs. He endeavoured to transform the preju-dices and superstitions of the people, emphasizing that ritualistic practices and external forms of worship kept the seeker of God away from the truth.

Herbert, George (1593–1633)   Herbert was a Welsh poet, ora-tor and priest. Born into an artistic and wealthy family, he held prominent positions at Cambridge University and in Parliament, before he gave up his career to take holy orders in the Church of England. Throughout his life he wrote religious poems charac-terized by a precision of language, a metrical versatility, and an ingenious use of imagery that was favoured by the metaphysical school of poets. He is best remembered as a writer of poems and the hymn *"Come, My Way, My Truth, My Life."*

Jagat Singh (1884–1951)   Born in the village of Nussi not far from Beas, Punjab, Maharaj Jagat Singh was initiated when he was twenty-six years old by Maharaj Sawan Singh. Following his retirement in 1943 as vice-principal of the Punjab Agricultural College, he spent the remainder of his life in his Master's service at Beas. In 1948 Sardar Bahadur Jagat Singh was appointed by his Master to be his successor. *The Science of the Soul*, a compilation of his discourses and excerpts from his letters to seekers and disciples, was published after his passing.

Kabir (c.1398–1518)   Born in Kashi (Banaras or Varanasi), Kabir Sahib eked out a meagre living weaving cloth. Teaching the practice of the Word, he travelled throughout India and attracted a large following of disciples, Hindus as well as Muslims. Kabir faced unrelenting opposition from the priestly class for his outspoken condemnation of rituals and the outward show of religion. Today, his verses are still popular and frequently quoted throughout India, and the versatility and power of his poetry are widely acknowledged.

Mahavira (599–527 BCE)   Mahavira is the name most commonly used to refer to the Indian sage Vardhamana who established what are today considered to be the central tenets of Jainism. According to Jain tradition, he was the 24th and the last Tirthankara. He devoted his life to preaching the eternal truth of spiritual freedom to people around India. His preaching and efforts to spread Jain philosophy is considered the real catalyst to the spread of this ancient religion throughout India.

Mariechild, Diane is the author of *Mother Wit* and *Inner Dance*. She leads workshops and lectures frequently on women and Buddhism.

Maulana Rum (1207–1273)   Jalaluddin Rumi, known respectfully in India as Maulana Rum (the learned man of Rum), was of Persian origin from Balkh. He moved to Konya, Turkey, where he became a religious teacher. There he met Shams-i-Tabrez and became his disciple. Rumi wrote the *Masnavi* and *Diwan-i Shams-i Tabrez*, both of which have contributed to his contemporary status as one of the most well-known Sufi mystics and poets, popular in both the East and the West.

Mother Teresa (1910–1997)   An Albanian Roman Catholic nun with Indian citizenship, Agnes Gonxha Bojaxhiu, better known as

Mother Teresa, founded the Missionaries of Charity in Kolkata, India, in 1950. For over 45 years she ministered to the poor, sick, orphaned, and dying, while guiding the Missionaries of Charity's expansion, first throughout India and then in other countries. She won the *Nobel Peace Prize* in 1979 and India's highest civilian honour, the *Bharat Ratna*, in 1980 for her humanitarian work.

Naidu, Sarojini (1879–1949)   Also known as the *Nightingale of India*, Sarojini Naidu was a child prodigy, freedom fighter, and poet. Naidu was the first Indian woman to become the President of the Indian National Congress and the first woman to become the Governor of the state of Uttar Pradesh. She was active in the Indian Independence Movement, joining Mahatma Gandhi in the Salt March to Dandi, and then leading the Dharasana Satyagraha after Gandhi was arrested. She herself was arrested and jailed several times during the freedom struggle.

Nehru, Jawaharlal (1889–1964)   Jawaharlal Nehru was a major political leader, a freedom fighter, a pivotal figure in the Congress Party, and the first and longest-serving prime minister of independent India, serving from 1947 to 1964. Both as prime minister and as Congress president, Nehru pushed through India's Parliament a series of legal reforms intended to emancipate women and bring equality. These reforms include raising the minimum marriageable age from twelve to fifteen, empowering women to divorce their husbands and inherit property, and declaring illegal the dowry system. His tenure was instrumental in shaping the traditions and structures of independent India and he is often referred to as the 'Architect of Modern India'.

Philokalia   *Philokalia* is a collection of texts written between the fourth and fifteenth centuries by spiritual masters of the Orthodox Christian tradition.

Qur'an   The *Qur'an* is the sacred scripture of Islam, written in Arabic, and understood to be revealed to the Prophet Muhammad in the beginning of the 7th century. It consists of 114 chapters covering many different topics – sacred, legal, social and scientific.

Ravidas   Guru Ravidas was a well-known saint who lived in Kashi and traveled across Rajasthan and other parts of India. He was a contemporary of Kabir and is believed to be a disciple of Swami Ramanand. Born into a Hindu family, he supported himself by making and repairing shoes and had a great impact on the many people who came to him for spiritual guidance, including Princess Mira Bai and Raja Pipa. Some of his writings are preserved in the *Adi Granth*.

Sen, Amartya (1933–)   Dr Amartya Sen, born in Shanti Niketan, West Bengal, is a distinguished economist-philosopher known for his contributions to welfare economics. He has worked in the areas of famine, human development theory, and the underlying mechanisms of poverty, gender equality and political liberalism. He won the *Nobel Memorial Prize in Economic Sciences* in 1998 and the *Bharat Ratna*, India's highest civilian honour, in 1999. From 1998 to 2004 he was Master of Trinity College at Cambridge University, becoming the first Asian academic to head an Oxbridge college. He is currently the Thomas W. Lamont University Professor and Professor of Economics and Philosophy at Harvard University. He has over 80 honorary doctorates from renowned universities worldwide.

Tagore, Rabindranath (1861–1941)   Tagore was a Bengali poet, visual artist, playwright, novelist and composer whose work received world-wide acclaim. He became Asia's first Nobel laureate when he won the 1913 *Nobel Prize in Literature*. At the age of sixteen, he published his first substantial poetry under the pseudonym *Bhanushingho ("Sun Lion")* and wrote his first short stories and dramas in 1877. In later life Tagore protested strongly against the British Raj and gave his support to the Indian Independence Movement. Tagore's life work endures in the form of his poetry and the institution he founded, Visva-Bharati University. Tagore wrote novels, short stories, songs, dance-dramas, and essays on political and personal topics. *Gitanjali (Song Offerings)*, *Gora (Fair-Faced)*, and *Ghare-Baire (The Home and the World)* are among his best-known works.

Tao Te Ching   It is difficult to know much for certain about the origins of the Tao Te Ching *(The Book of the Way and Its Power)*, a fundamental Taoist text that espouses the way of the Tao, the timeless ultimate principle, which is followed through simplicity, humility, and non-binding action. The Tao Te Ching was probably compiled before the latter half of the third century BC, but it is thought that the book is based on Chinese oral tradition that may even antedate the written word. The author of the *Tao Te Ching* is commonly referred to as Lao-Tzu or Lao Tse (there are many variants in English), but modern scholars doubt that he actually existed. It is probable that 'Lao-Tzu', which means both 'the old philosopher' and 'the old philosophy', refers to the ancient origin of the varied material within the text.

Teilhard de Chardin, Pierre (1881–1955)   Teilhard was a French philosopher and Jesuit priest who trained as a palaeontologist and geologist and participated in the discovery of Peking Man. He conceived the idea of the Omega Point and developed Vladimir Vernadsky's concept of Noosphere. Teilhard's primary book, *The Phenomenon of Man*, set forth a sweeping account of the unfolding of the cosmos. He abandoned traditional interpretations of creation in the biblical book of *Genesis* in favour of a less strict interpretation. This displeased certain officials in the Roman Curia, who thought that it undermined the doctrine of original sin developed by Saint Augustine. Teilhard's position was opposed by his church superiors, and his work was denied publication during his lifetime by the Roman Holy Office.

Washington, George (1732–1799)   George Washington was a surveyor, farmer and soldier who rose to become the Commander in Chief of the Continental army during the American Revolution and first president of the United States (1789–97). He is called "the father of his country" for his crucial role in fighting for, creating and leading the United States of America in its earliest days. He presided over the Philadelphia Convention that drafted the United States Constitution in 1787. Washington has been consistently ranked by scholars as one of the greatest USA Presidents.

Weiss, Brian L. M.D.   Dr. Weiss is an American psychiatrist who graduated from Yale University School of Medicine. He is currently Chairman Emeritus of the Department of Psychiatry at Mount Sinai Medical Center in Miami and Clinical Associate Professor of Psychiatry at University of Miami School of Medicine. He is the author of seven books on the subject of reincarnation, including the best-seller, *Only Love is Real*.

Williamson, Marianne (1952–)   Williamson is a spiritual activist, author, lecturer and founder of the Peace Alliance, a grassroots campaign supporting legislation currently before the USA Congress to establish a United States Department of Peace. She has published nine books, including four New York Times #1 Bestsellers. Her books include: *Imagine What America Could Be in the 21st Century: Visions of a Better Future from Leading American Thinkers, Healing the Soul of America: Reclaiming our Voices as Spiritual Citizens,* and *A Woman's Worth*.

This book has been prepared by the sangat of Radha Soami Satsang Beas, www.RSSB.org, a registered charitable society dedicated to dissemination of spiritual understanding and values.